WHAT ARE YOU THIRSTY FOR?

WHAT ARE YOU THIRSTY FOR?

Rethinking
alcohol and
the life
you want

ANNA DONAGHEY

To my husband Kieran.
You always saw the version of me that was still on her way.
Thank you for waiting while I caught up.

Published in 2026 by New River Books
Unit 105, Leroy House, 436 Essex Road, London N1 3QP
www.newriverbooks.co.uk

10 9 8 7 6 5 4 3 2 1

Copyright © Anna Donaghey 2026

The author has asserted her right under the Copyright, Designs and Patents Act 1988 to be identified as the author of this work. All rights reserved. No part of this publication may be reproduced, stored in a retrieval system or transmitted in any form, or by any means (electronic, mechanical, or otherwise) without the prior written permission of both the copyright owners and the publisher.

A CIP catalogue record for this book is available from the British Library.

ISBN: 978-1-915780-60-7

Illustrations on pages 46, 69, 95, 108, 137, 185, 196 and 241 by Hannah Wilson, Quoted Visually
Illustrations on pages 11, 72, 107, 128, and 148 by Rob Brandt

Printed and bound in the UK using 100% Renewable Electricity at CPI Group (UK) Ltd, Croydon CR0 4YY. This FSC© label means that materials used for the product have been responsibly sourced.

Where images or quotes have been used in this text, every effort has been made to contact copyright holders and abide by 'fair use' guidelines. If you are a copyright holder and wish to get in touch, please email info@newriverbooks.co.uk

CONTENTS

Introduction		9
1	Awareness, not absolutes	16
2	The jobs we give alcohol to do	23
3	The big sell	50
4	The trouble with Swiss Army Knives	68
5	Habit, dependency & the grey area in-between	88
6	The great disconnect	102
7	The happiness myth	124
8	Seeing the full picture	142
9	Why change feels hard (and how to make it easier)	166
10	Rewiring habits	190
11	Sacking the CEO	208
12	What are you thirsty for?	236

INTRODUCTION

What are you thirsty for?

Not just physically, but in your life. Comfort? Connection? Relief? Freedom? We all have cravings, and we all reach for something to satisfy them. For years, I reached for alcohol. I didn't question why; it was just what I did. But when I finally stopped drinking, I realised alcohol had never really been quenching my thirst. It had just kept me thirsty for more.

I used to work in the advertising industry. My job was to uncover the deep, unspoken desires that drive people's decisions: what motivates them? What makes them feel seen, understood and valued? What products do they believe will make them happy?

The truth is, we don't just buy products. We buy stories. Stories about who we are, who we could be, and what we need to feel whole. For years, I helped sell some of the biggest brands in the world, including alcoholic drinks. And what I regret most now, looking back, is that I helped sell a story about drinking that I would later myself fight to unlearn.

My official job title was Strategist – which I liked the sound of, but my colleagues liked to ground me by calling me 'Anna the Planner'. It doesn't sound quite as fancy but I guess it does have a certain ring to it.

Either way, my job was to bring insight to the table – to be nosey, if you like, about how people behaved, what they needed, and what they hankered for in life. Often considered 'the clever ones' in an agency, Strategists were tasked with taking these nuggets of killer insight and crafting them into a brief for the Creatives, or 'the arty-farty ones'. They in turn would use this to come up with campaigns that spoke to people in distinctive, memorable and persuasive ways. And which always had a common goal: to encourage people to lean into a message, and respond accordingly.

Buy this make of car. Travel by that particular airline. Eat this brand of crisps. Join that like-minded community. Start doing X. Stop doing Y.

My insights shaped campaigns for well-known brands across industries – from cars (sexy!) to toilet bleach (less sexy!) to alcohol. But what truly excited me was working on healthcare brands and campaigns that could genuinely enhance a consumer or patient's life.

One of the reasons that Strategists often convey an air of (pseudo-) intelligence is because we love a framework. In fact, models and frameworks are our thing. Getting up in a meeting to sketch a model of consumer behaviour as if it had just popped into my head instilled confidence in my audience that I knew what I was talking about. And one model that I whipped out more frequently than any other was the Trans-Theoretical Model, a fancy-pants name for a simple concept: the five stages of behaviour change, from recognising 'a problem' to making lasting change.

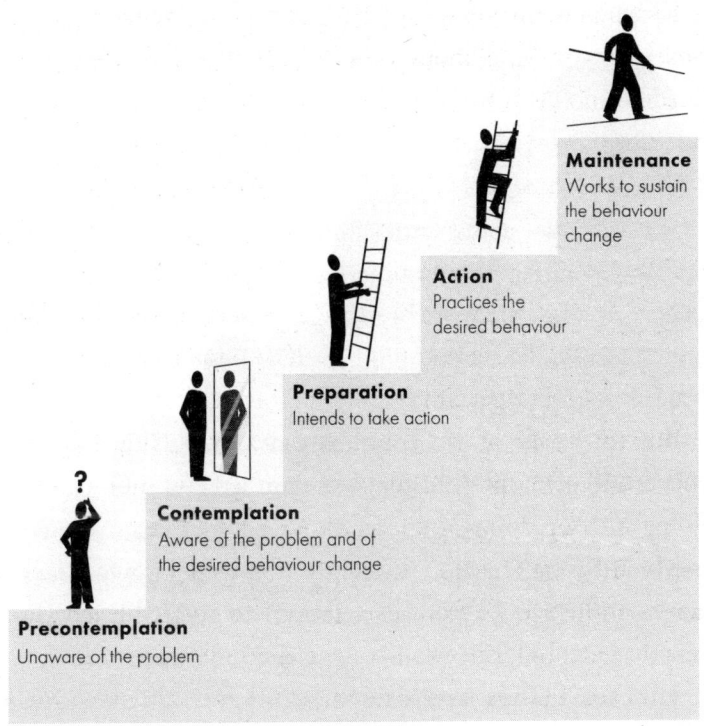

Understanding this model was fundamental in my work, but it became even more significant when I realised I had been stuck in the first stage myself for years – completely unaware of my own escalating drinking problem. I'll explore this more later in the book, but for now, the key takeaway is this:

People don't change all at once. Change happens in stages, and the first step isn't action – it's awareness.

I used to think drinking was just a normal part of life. Over time, though, for me – and I can't pinpoint when – it stopped feeling like a choice and started feeling like something I had to do. And, for years, I stayed stuck. Not because I didn't want to change, but because I didn't believe I could.

The process of breaking free wasn't about willpower, labels, or rules. It was about curiosity. It was about stepping back and asking different questions – just like the little dude in the diagram, scratching his head. Not only different questions about alcohol, but also about myself. And that's what this book is here to help you do.

This isn't a book about quitting drinking. There are lots of 'get sober' books available, and they tend to get picked up by people who've already decided that they want (or very commonly, need) to quit booze – perhaps their life has begun to unravel in some way, relationships have been compromised or damaged, or simply things have got too much.

It's a book about rethinking drinking.

It's not a 'How to…' book.

It's a 'What if…?' book.

A book about questioning what alcohol is really doing for you, and what life could feel like without it.

It's about understanding what you're seeking, and whether alcohol is helping you find it, or keeping it just out of reach.

So, let's start at the beginning. Not with the problem, but with a question: *What are you thirsty for?*

PART 1

AWARENESS

CHAPTER 1

AWARENESS, NOT ABSOLUTES

When I became an alcohol mindset coach, I stepped into a world where sobriety was often framed as a transformation, and spoken about with near-religious fervour. I met people who were not just alcohol-free but evangelical about it, convinced that life only truly begins on the other side of drinking. In some spaces, I encountered a rigid 'us vs. them' mentality, where drinkers were seen as blind, misguided, or even in denial, while non-drinkers were the enlightened ones.

This binary thinking never sat comfortably with me.

I don't believe that alcohol needs to be demonised, nor do I believe that sobriety needs to be put on a pedestal. Drinking is a deeply personal choice, and my goal has never been to tell people what they should or shouldn't do. As a coach, it is no more my place to tell people whether they should drink or not, than it is for me to tell them what colour pants to wear.

My mission is awareness, not absolutes. I want to help people see alcohol clearly, and strip away cultural conditioning, so that they can make fully conscious, individual choices about its role in their lives.

I long for a world where drinking – or not drinking – stops being a defining trait. Where the labels of 'drinker' and 'non-drinker' dissolve, and instead, we all just exist in a space of informed decision-making. A world where alcohol is not loaded with societal expectation, guilt or identity, but is seen for what it is: a substance and a choice. Not a position, or status.

I'm optimistic that we are moving in that direction, and in 2024 I launched The Big Drink Rethink podcast. I wanted a platform from which to explore the shift and to celebrate the fact that change is afoot. And, through my own exploration, I realised I could give listeners plenty of food for thought in terms of what alcohol might personally mean to them.

Much like the podcast, I want this book to stand as a conduit of awareness, rather than an arbiter of judgment. It's not here to preach, to divide, or to tell you what is right for you. It's here to illuminate, to prompt reflection, and to give you the space to decide, on your own terms, whether alcohol deserves the role it currently plays in your life.

Because true freedom is not about abstinence or indulgence. It's about clarity. And awareness. Once you have that, you can choose with power, rather than from a sense of pressure.

A CURIOUS EXHIBIT

Back in the day, before I decided that there just wasn't enough booze involved, I often used to visit art galleries. I lived in London, which of course meant that there were lots to choose from. On the weekend I loved nothing more than taking the scenic route from my flat in Hammersmith, to whichever exhibition I had chosen to visit. I would make my way, criss-crossing the many bridges along the River Thames on my vintage scooter, soaking up the London landscape and the city vibes. Back when I still felt high on life and the possibilities felt endless.

I loved galleries, particularly the more modern ones, with their light, bright, interactive spaces. I like the way they enable you to step outside your daily life and just focus on whatever they are showcasing.

Let's imagine, for a moment, stepping into such a place.

The lighting is soft, the air is quiet. You're here for a special exhibition, which promises to be deeply personal and fascinating. It is an exhibition about alcohol. As you enter the space, you see a large exhibit in the centre of the room – 'Alcohol: A Cultural Artifact'. It isn't one object, but a mosaic – fragmented and layered. All around, projections flicker on the walls: scenes where alcohol is playing a central role.

It's a representation of alcohol not so much as a drink, or a social ritual, but as an idea – a symbol, storyteller and shape-shifter. This is your opportunity to explore alcohol as you've never encountered it before. A chance to withdraw your participation, leave your assumptions, habits and judgements behind. In this exhibition, you are merely an observer.

You are able to ponder alcohol, wander around it and examine it from all angles. Little prompts encourage you to imagine its history, its role in celebrations and sorrows, its promises and its pitfalls. Your imagination is allowed to run away with the stories it holds, the moments it has witnessed, and the ways it has influenced lives across centuries.

And oh my goodness, has it been around for a long time! A timeline stretching back thousands of years showcases alcohol as an ancient 'elixir', crafted and brewed by those seeking connection and celebration. There are paintings of feasts and banquets. You can imagine the laughter ringing through ancient halls, the toasts to victories, community and companionship.

You move on to the next room. The first display comprises brightly lit shelves, lined with sleek bottles and eye-catching advertisements. Alluring slogans promise relaxation, fun, kinship and sophistication. But then next to them, another display, less well illuminated, paints a rather different picture. Peering at the contents, you see that it contains statistics, testimonies, and warnings. Stories of lives changed, moments missed, ambitions squashed and potential unrealised. It feels at odds with the spot-lit, polished bottles, and you pause to consider the tension between the two displays.

Proceeding on through the exhibition, you enter a room where there are smaller alcoves, each containing exhibits that focus on a different angle of the story. There's one that showcases how alcohol is perceived in different cultures. Another explores the economics of alcohol, highlighting how its production and sale have shaped industries and communities. Another, with magnified images of cells and organs, tells a visual story about how alcohol affects the body; and yet another showcases the effects that alcohol has on the brain and mental health. Each exhibit invites you to linger, to learn, and to think about the meanings beyond the surface.

And, finally, there's a mirrored room. It is empty save for prompts encouraging you to reflect on your own experiences with alcohol. How big a part does alcohol play in your story? When and where does it show up? Has it been a guest at your happiest moments, adding warmth to celebrations? Or has it cast shadows in your hardest times, whispering promises of escape that came with costs?

With so much to take in and reflect upon, there is no rush. A seating area allows you to plonk yourself down and absorb what you've seen. This isn't a place for judgement or conclusions. Just an opportunity to look, learn, wonder and ruminate. As you leave the exhibition, you walk underneath an exit sign, that invites you to carry that spirit of curiosity with you as you go on your way.

If you've ever listened to The Big Drink Rethink podcast, you'll recognise 'curiosity' as a word that I utter often. Because, much like in that exhibition, it transforms the familiar into the fascinating, and the unquestioned into the examined. It invites us to see our choices and surroundings with fresh eyes – so that in that moment, we are not just thinking about alcohol, we are rethinking it.

rethink

[verb or noun: ree-thingk]

Verb: To think again about a plan, idea or system in order to change or improve it.

Noun: The act of thinking again about something to reassess or reconsider it.

(Source: The Oxford English Dictionary)

In my advertising life, my role demanded that I was deeply curious about what makes people tick, but I also know that curiosity is how we grow.

Curiosity is the key to knowledge, and knowledge is power. Quite simply, the more we understand, the more control we have over our choices and our future. When we're armed with the right information, we're no longer at the mercy of old habits or assumptions. Instead, we are in the driver's seat, making decisions that truly serve us. It's not just about learning facts; it's about gaining the clarity and confidence to create a life we love, one choice at a time.

KEY TAKE-AWAYS:

- Most people never truly examine their relationship with alcohol; they simply accept it as part of life.
- Looking at alcohol from multiple angles, like an exhibit in a gallery, allows us to step back and see it in a new light.
- The goal is to move from autopilot to awareness, and to challenge what we've been conditioned to believe.
- The more we educate ourselves, the more we can make intentional choices rather than default ones.

Food for thought:

1. **Have you ever paused to ask why alcohol has the place it does in your life?**

   Have you made conscious decisions along the way – or is it something that has just happened?

2. **If you were to view alcohol as an 'exhibit' – a cultural artifact rather than a given – what would you notice?**
   How has it been presented to you through society, the media, and personal experiences?

3. **What assumptions about alcohol have you inherited from your environment?**
   Which beliefs feel like your own, and which ones more the result of conditioning?

4. **What emotions arise when you think about alcohol's presence in your life?**
   Does it bring a sense of joy, connection, relaxation, or something more complex?

5. **What would it mean for you to approach alcohol with genuine curiosity?**
   If you set aside judgement or pressure, what questions are you now willing to ask yourself?

Related podcast episodes:
Episode 1. What The Big Drink Rethink is All About
Episode 2. Exploring our Love Affair with Alcohol
Episode 12. Crafting a New Drinking Narrative
Episode 36. Breaking Down Silos in Alcohol Culture

CHAPTER 2

THE JOBS WE GIVE ALCOHOL TO DO

For many, alcohol would appear to play a positive role. Let me just get that out there. The majority of adults drink it, and most do not come to struggle with it like I did. Indeed many would say that the social interactions it lubricates add to their lives. And science backs this up: our brains are wired for connection, and drinking eases this in a way that can contribute greatly to our happiness. Social interactions boost feel-good chemicals like dopamine and oxytocin, helping us feel seen, safe and supported. And this social interaction and sense of community isn't just comforting; it's a biological need that helps combat loneliness and promote lasting joy – which is perhaps why most health medics rarely totally condemn alcohol.

In one of the earliest episodes of The Big Drink Rethink podcast, I spoke with David Nutt, a world-renowned Professor of Neuropsychopharmacology and former top drugs adviser to the UK government. He explained why alcohol has been, throughout history, the most social of drugs: 'What alcohol does, essentially, is dampen social anxiety. Humans are genetically wired to be slightly wary of others. It is a survival instinct. Being cautious rather than overly familiar helped our ancestors avoid potential threats. But alcohol increases a brain chemical called GABA, which reduces anxiety and allows us to relax and connect with others. That's why alcohol has long been a social lubricant. It helps us feel at ease, fostering conviviality and connection at parties, gatherings and first meetings.'

Herein lies a seldom-considered truth. Alcohol is a drug. A psychoactive drug, which means it changes the way we think, feel and behave. It slows down the central nervous system, making us feel more relaxed, less anxious, and more confident. As David says, it increases the effects of GABA, a brain chemical that calms us down; and at the same time it reduces the effects of glutamate, a neurotransmitter that normally keeps us alert. The result? Lowered inhibitions, a sense of ease, and sometimes a boost in mood. That's why alcohol plays such a key role in social settings – it makes people feel more open, talkative, less self-conscious, and even more creative.

When people feel more connected, ideas flow freely – it's easy to see why alcohol has been intertwined with the building of societies, cultural movements, and even great innovations.

A TRUSTED PERSONAL ASSISTANT

Of course, we don't just drink alcohol to grease social dynamics. We give it many jobs to do. And typically, those jobs boil down to one simple idea: we want to feel more of a positive emotion and less of a negative one:

- More relaxed, less stressed.
- Calmer, less anxious.
- More confident, less self-conscious.
- More fun, less dull.

And because alcohol seems to deliver on these promises, we rarely question it. We treat it like a trusted Personal Assistant whom we can always rely on to show up and get the job done.

We believe it works, and that belief sits at the very core of our relationship with it, shaping our thoughts and driving what we do. Because our behaviours don't just appear out of nowhere. They're driven by a simple but powerful – and often subconscious – cycle:

$$\text{Beliefs} \rightarrow \text{Thoughts} \rightarrow \text{Actions}$$

It's a thought pattern that shows up everywhere in life, e.g.

- If we believe it's a dog-eat-dog world, we'll think of life as a competition, and we probably won't act like a team player.
- If we believe experience only comes with age, we'll assume we're too young for that management role, and we won't even apply.

And it's exactly the same with alcohol:
- If we believe alcohol helps us relax, we'll think of it when we're stressed, and we'll pour ourselves a drink.
- If we believe alcohol makes us more socially confident, we'll think of it before a party, and have a quick drink before heading out.

We're literally asking alcohol to help us:
- 'Alcohol, please help me relax.'
- 'Alcohol, please help me feel more confident.'

And it doesn't stop there:
- 'Please help me sleep.'
- 'Please help me feel happier.'
- 'Please help me feel less bored… less lonely… more sexy… more interesting… more connected.'

Bit by bit, drink by drink, we hand over these jobs to alcohol, trusting it to deliver.

Over time, our loyalty to this Personal Assistant deepens. As we move through different life stages – into new environments, which trigger different needs and create different emotional states – so our relationship with alcohol adapts and changes. And society backs this relationship up at every turn. From celebration to commiseration, from social bonding to stress relief, alcohol weaves itself into the fabric of our lives, marking every milestone, transition and pivotal event.

And when a drug becomes so normalised that we rarely

question it, it's worth asking ourselves: is alcohol just a useful social lubricant in my life? Or has it become more than that – a way of easing my thoughts and boosting my mood in a more general way?

Let's look at how alcohol accompanies us on our life journey.

1. Early adulthood

For a teenager, drinking is about social bonding and belonging – alcohol is a symbol of adulthood.

When at 15, I sat in my boyfriend's garden, sipping Blue Curaçao, cigarette in hand, The Smiths playing in the background, I wasn't just drinking, I was defining myself.

Through university and my early working life, alcohol was a social lubricant, and a passport to connection. It reassured me that I fitted in, that I was fun, that I belonged.

At this stage in life, we tend to ask alcohol to smooth out awkwardness, loosen our inhibitions, and help us find our place in the crowd. The world, even. But beneath the surface, the real job we're giving it is validation. Looking back now, I can see that my drinking in those early years wasn't just about having fun. It was about proving something. Proving that I was up for a laugh. That I was fun to be around.

Beliefs: Alcohol = confidence, popularity, social success.

2. Career & work culture

As much as we might try to avoid responsibility, sooner or later, reality kicks in. We have to figure out what we want to do with our lives, land a job and start earning a living. And if we're ambitious, we might also want to stand out, climb the career ladder, and prove ourselves as quickly as possible.

As we step into the working world, alcohol is no longer just about fun.

My first job after university was in manufacturing, working for Rover, the car company that once dominated South Birmingham. In those days, it felt like everyone had a connection to 'The Rover'. It was an institution, employing thousands. Fridays were an early finish for those on the factory floor, and when the car assembly blocks emptied, workers poured into the local pubs in Longbridge to celebrate the end of the week and the start of the weekend. And me? I was the girl with the posh-sounding accent, going pint for pint with my Brummie track worker colleagues. I loved it. I felt kinship. I felt accepted.

After eight years at 'The Rover', I moved to London and found my way into the fast-paced, high-energy world of advertising. This time, it wasn't just after-work pints. Alcohol was ingrained in the industry. The agencies I worked for even had bars inside the building. But if they hadn't, we were in Soho, where there was a pub on every corner. Meetings happened over drinks, lunches with clients stretched long into the afternoon, and most evenings ended in bars and restaurants near the office before I made my way home. I travelled the world with colleagues, passed through airport lounges on a weekly basis, and stayed in beautiful hotels. Alcohol was everywhere and, effectively, free. The expense account covered pretty much everything. I had incredibly close relationships with my colleagues. They weren't just co-workers – to this single girl in her late twenties/early thirties, they felt like my extended family. And in this family, alcohol was ever-present.

Beliefs: Alcohol = assimilation, professional bonding, career success, a job perk and relaxation.

3. Marriage, parenthood & settling down

Life keeps moving. By the time we hit our 30s, many of us start thinking about settling down. Marriage, homes and kids are on the agenda, and as always, alcohol is right there with us. It signifies joy, achievement, success. It's present at every major milestone: our birthdays, weddings, promotions, new homes, and, of course, the arrival of our little bundles of joy.

But this stage of life also brings whole new challenges. Careers, relationships and parenthood all demand more from us than ever before. And if there's one thing that changes everything, it's having children. The shift is seismic. Life, once centred around personal freedom, becomes an endless juggling act of responsibilities, sleep deprivation, and the quiet but relentless pressure to hold it all together.

And so, once again, the jobs we give alcohol to do evolve. It's no longer just a social lubricant or a way to celebrate or relax. Now, it becomes an escape hatch. A glass of wine after the kids are in bed, to signal that the day is finally over. Several glasses or a few beers while cooking dinner can become a ritual to smooth out the chaos – a small rebellion against the weight of responsibility. At this stage of life, alcohol's role becomes more private. It's not just about toasting life's big moments any more; it's about relieving the stress of a heavy working day, carving out a pocket of 'me time' in the relentless rush of adulting.

Beliefs = escape, a reward, self-care and validation.

4. Midlife

The big old chunk of time we label 'midlife' can encompass many transitions. This is where I currently am in life, as I sit and write, aged 54. I'm navigating my own version of middle-age, and someone else's might look and feel very different. But here are some common transitions during which alcohol can easily slip into the role of a coping mechanism (brace yourself, because if you're not there yet, this does not make midlife sound appealing. So let me say now that it is also a very rewarding time of life, but man, does it have its turbulence!):

- Career shifts: work life is rarely a totally trouble-free zone. At some point, a difficult boss or a progression ceiling may bring frustration or disappointment and challenge your sense of self-worth. Perhaps you find yourself under financial stress after being made redundant. Or you get burnt out. The stress of uncertainty, disappointment or a loss of identity connected to any of these scenarios can lead to an increased reliance on alcohol to alleviate feelings of inadequacy or a fear of the future, or simply

to unwind from the pressure.
- Divorce or relationship strain: marriage breakdown and relationship failures can cause intense emotional turmoil. The grief and loss associated with the end of a relationship can induce a whole range of painful emotions – sadness, anger and guilt, to name but a few. And in this scenario, we easily turn to alcohol as a way to numb them and provide a temporary escape from the heartache. Drinking may become a nightly ritual to manage feelings of loneliness or rejection, or to distract from apprehension about what the future holds.
- Empty nest syndrome: if you have children, you can experience a profound sense of loss when they leave home. Maybe you exited the workplace years ago to dedicate yourself to raising them, in which case big questions about your role and purpose may bubble up. Shifting home dynamics can make you feel empty and depressed – for which drinking can seem to provide a quick solution.
- 'Is this it?': we talk about people having a 'midlife crisis', and it's a very real and understandable thing. We can start to question our achievements, the choices we've made, our very identity… We might like to think we're impervious to such things, but midlife can bring a heightened awareness of societal expectations and the pressure to 'measure up' in terms of success and social status.
- A reckoning: midlife is often described like this – and for good reason. It's a time when old wounds can

resurface with surprising force. Family dynamics we've papered over, disappointments we've buried, traumas we've never fully processed – they all have a way of rising to the surface, demanding attention. This can happen at any stage of life, of course. But midlife has a particular potency: the dual weight of what has happened and what hasn't. The realisation that time is finite. The grief of unlived dreams. The guilt or shame we carry, often without even realising it.

- Trauma – especially the kind we've minimised or normalised – can feel like a shadow we've spent decades outrunning. Whether it's childhood neglect, emotional abandonment, loss, or the silent traumas of being unseen or unheard for too long, these experiences shape our nervous systems and beliefs in deep, invisible ways. Alcohol, in this context, isn't just a way to take the edge off. It becomes a tool for emotional containment. A way to push the pain down when we don't yet feel equipped to face it head-on.
- 'Sandwich generation' pressures: this refers to those of us simultaneously caring for our children and our aging parents, often while managing careers and other responsibilities. This is a tough gig. We are literally 'sandwiched' between two care-giving roles, with all the emotional, financial and physical stress that this rains down. My coaching clients who find themselves weighed down with these pressures talk about 'me time' moments of drinking alone 'to validate that I even exist when it feels like the entire world wants a piece of me'.

Beliefs = comfort, emotional suppression, distraction, protection and resilience.

5. Later life

As life moves on again, alcohol finds yet another role to play – this time, managing the heavier burdens that come with age. Personal illness, the decline of a loved one, chronic pain… these can be a stark reminder of mortality.

The psychological toll of aging can also make people feel disconnected from their past vitality. Suddenly, they feel a whole new kind of loneliness, and alcohol becomes a way to take the edge off. A glass of wine to quiet the racing thoughts. A whisky to take the sting out of grief. A drink to fill the silence.

Loneliness can affect anyone, of any age. Indeed, many consider it to be one of the greatest public health challenges we face in western societies.

According to the Campaign to End Loneliness, approximately 3.83 million adults in the UK experience chronic loneliness, meaning they feel lonely 'often or always'. But it is particularly debilitating for the elderly, and those suffering from it often add 'companionship' to the jobs asked of alcohol. The ritual of a nightly drink can bring a sense of routine or comfort in a time when life feels uncertain, unstimulating or empty.

Beliefs = coping, numbing, comfort and companionship.

AN EVER-EXPANDING JOB DESCRIPTION

Notice how alcohol's job description expands as life goes on. It rarely goes the other way. Once we assign it a role, it tends to stick. If it helped us form friendships in our youth, it often remains the glue that holds those friendships together later in life. It becomes woven into our shared history, the backdrop of our best stories and memories. Changing that dynamic can feel risky, like tampering with the foundation of something precious.

And, of course, once we've used alcohol as a social facilitator, stress reliever, emotional buffer, or a way to manage loneliness, it's hard to unlearn that pattern. Habit kicks in. Life keeps throwing new challenges our way. The need remains, so alcohol stays on in the role we originally hired it for. If alcohol were a person, we might even feel sorry for it, labouring away under an ever-expanding workload. Constantly having to pick up new responsibilities.

But the reality is, it's not just being overworked – it's being promoted.

What started out as a simple Personal Assistant, helping us navigate social settings, has now climbed the ranks. Slowly but surely, it's been handed more and more tasks, and become something much bigger: our Chief Emotions Officer.

Come to think of it, every single job we give alcohol is tied to managing emotions. More confidence, less self-doubt. More ease, less stress. More joy, less sadness. And the more jobs we give it, the more essential it seems. What began as a social drug has now taken on the role of self-medication.

NEVER FEELING ENOUGH

'Do you ever think about harming yourself?' the therapist asked.

I shifted uncomfortably in my chair, my eyes flicking towards the half-open window. Outside, the world carried on as usual: the sound of footsteps, laughter, conversations drifting up from the street below.

A street full of normal people.

People not like me.

What was their secret? How did they hold it together so effortlessly while I felt like I was constantly unravelling?

I forced my attention back to her question. She watched me closely, waiting. For a second, she thought I hadn't heard her. Then, with a slight, barely perceptible tilt of her head, she urged me to answer.

I could have told her the truth. I could have said that sometimes, when I was driving, I'd briefly wonder how easy it would be to drift into oncoming traffic. Not because I wanted to die. Just because I felt exhausted by the constant, suffocating 'What ifs?' running wild in my brain.

I decided not to share. Not because I was actively planning anything; in fact, it wasn't the action that haunted me – it was the possibility. The relentless fragility of life. The feeling that I was constantly at the mercy of forces beyond my control.

I felt so fucking vulnerable. All the time.

A deep sense of shame swallowed me whole. No way was I about to admit this to the woman sitting across from me. And I certainly wasn't going to spill the beans about how much I was drinking just to quiet my thoughts.

In fact, this whole therapy thing was making me more uncomfortable by the second. I wanted out. I wanted to be at home, curled up with a bottle of wine, letting the numbness wash over me.

How the hell had I got here?

I drank to relieve stress, to fit in, to be sociable, to suppress loneliness, to relieve boredom, to reduce sadness, bring happiness.

There was always a reason to drink.

And here I was, trapped in my own 15-year pity party, self-medicating with alcohol and feeding a stealth-like addiction.

Despite having a circle of amazing family and friends, I felt completely alone. Despite having a successful career, I felt like a failure.

'Do you ever think about harming yourself?' she asked again.

My answer should have been that I was tearing strips off myself every single day and didn't know how to stop. Instead, I just shook my head.

'No,' I said. 'I'm fine.'

It would be another ten years before I took action on my drinking.

Ten more years of convincing myself I was fine.

Ten more years of shaming myself every single day.

Ten more years of pretending I was happier than I really was.

By the time I finally admitted that I wasn't fine, that I was, in fact, far from fine, I was utterly exhausted. Not just from the drinking itself, but from the sheer weight of keeping up the illusion that everything was okay.

BELIEFS THAT SHAPE OUR DRINKING

I used to think that if I could just drink less, everything would fall into place. That if I could just get my relationship with alcohol under control, everything else would make sense.

But when I finally started doing the work, I realised that controlling my drinking was only half the equation.

Because the real reason I was drinking wasn't just about alcohol.

It was about me.

It was about what I believed about myself.

And when I started unpicking that, everything changed.

1988: The snigger

I was 17. A bundle of teenage hormones wrapped in angsty defiance.

My brother was off to Oxford University, and my parents, keen to offer equal opportunities, thought I might follow in his footsteps. With the best of intentions, they encouraged me to sit the Oxbridge entrance exam in the run-up to my A-Levels.

I didn't want to. My brother was a straight-A student; I, quite frankly, was not. I spent far more time hanging out with my boyfriend (he of the exotic drinks cabinet) than studying, and I was already convinced my basic A-Levels had disaster written all over them. The idea of sitting an additional paper for one of the most prestigious universities in the country? Absurd.

I don't remember it being the kind of exam you could actually study for. It was more about abstract thinking than factual regurgitation. Either way, because I didn't want to take it, I did very little to prepare.

The day arrived. I turned over the exam paper and read the question: 'Is a dream a lie if it don't come true, or is it something worse? Discuss.'

I blinked.

Wait. What?

For a fleeting moment, delight swept over me. This was a lyric from 'The River' – my favourite song, by my favourite artist, Bruce Springsteen. If I could have picked a line from any song in the world, it would have been this one.

And yet, as quickly as that spark of recognition came, it disappeared.

I had nothing.

I had sung along to that song a thousand times, but never once had I considered the philosophical implications of Brucie's question. And now, faced with a blank page and an expectant clock, I froze.

Crickets.

Caught off-guard and completely unprepared, I managed to scrawl out about four measly lines. Four completely inadequate, mortifying lines.

The longest, most excruciating hour of my life dragged on,

and then it was over. The adjudicator walked the classroom floor, collecting papers. I handed mine over, already burning with embarrassment at how little I had written.

And then, as if to put the final nail in the coffin, he sniggered.

I have never felt shame and ridicule like it.

Fortunately, my regard for Springsteen remained intact. He can do no wrong. It wasn't his fault I felt like a complete fuck-up.

But my regard for myself?

That was shattered.

The birth of a limiting belief

A belief was born in me that that day: I'm not smart enough.

It settled deep inside me, like ink sinking into paper.

Limiting beliefs, the insidious kind, are the ones that tell us we are not enough. They're not always loud or dramatic. Sometimes, they whisper. They lurk in the background, shaping the way we see ourselves, subtly steering the course of our lives.

These beliefs are characterised by the 'I'm nots', the 'I can'ts', and the 'It's not possibles':

I'm not smart enough.

I'm not worthy enough.

I'm not capable enough.

And remember, that beliefs create thoughts, and thoughts drive behaviour.

If you believe you're not smart enough, you'll spend a

lifetime trying to compensate. Which is exactly what I did.

Living under punishing expectations

That single moment, the exam, the shame, the snigger, became a turning point I didn't even realise had happened. From that day forward, my internal script was rewritten:

> Belief: I'm not smart enough.
> Thoughts: I must try harder.
> Actions: Overwork, over-prepare, strive for perfection, seek external validation.

For 30 years, that belief around my own inadequacies drove a quest for perfectionism that was exhausting. It followed me around, and crept into every aspect of my life. I chased unachievable, high standards that shaped how I worked, how I interacted, how I saw myself.

At work, it showed up as relentless acts of striving to impress – which, let's be clear, is not the same as striving for excellence. Impressing others became my addiction. Recognition became my currency. My self-worth lived in the approval of others.

I over-prepared for meetings. I overcomplicated and polished my work until I had squeezed the life out of it. I hesitated to share ideas unless they were fully formed and bulletproof. I would sit in board meetings, waiting, analysing, crafting the perfect contribution – because, God forbid, I was shown up.

In my personal life, the same patterns played out. I

overthought, over-tweaked, and over-managed everything, suffocating the joy from even the simplest moments.

When I became a mother in my mid-30s, I felt completely out of my depth, like I'd been dropped into a foreign country without a map. A lot of women feel this way. But for me, it wasn't just the exhaustion or the relentless responsibility.

It was that voice whispering: See? You're not smart enough for this either.

I watched other mothers glide through it effortlessly. Calm, capable, their babies content, their nappy bags stocked, their hair brushed. I compared myself ruthlessly. I searched for that elusive maternal instinct that was supposed to just kick in. But I couldn't find it.

I found the monotony of maternity leave awful. The same routine day in, day out. The feeds, the nappy changes, the endless pacing in the dead of night. I adored my daughter, but I felt like I was disappearing inside my own life.

I resented my husband for getting to leave the house, for having a purpose beyond our four walls. I missed my career, my sense of self, my old life.

And so, I told myself a story: I'm not cut out for this. I don't have what it takes to be a good mum.

And then came the shame.

Because what kind of mother longs for escape? What kind of mother feels trapped by the very thing she's supposed to cherish?

I didn't just feel lost. I felt wrong.

All because, deep down, I was still carrying that 17-year-old girl inside me. The one who believed she wasn't smart enough.

The one who froze in front of an exam paper. The one who heard someone snigger and let it define her.

A 30-year testimony to the power of a single, unchallenged belief.

THE SLOW CREEP OF DEPENDENCE

I was 36 when I had my first daughter. By then, my 20-year relationship with alcohol had shifted.

I wasn't drinking for fun any more. Alcohol wasn't just a habit; it was my coping mechanism and my reward. The thing that got me through the day and the prize I gave myself at night.

The tsunami of emotions connected to motherhood was unlike anything I had ever experienced. The stress, the seismic shift in identity. It was a flood on an entirely new level.

I felt overwhelmed, trapped, desperate for a glimpse of the old me. So I gave alcohol another job: escape.

'Me time.'

I had thought I was ready for this new chapter. That after years of bottomless drinks in Soho bars, I was done. Motherhood was going to be my clean slate.

But about three months after my daughter was born, I was drinking a bottle of wine a night. I'd pump milk before drinking, then dump the next few feeds in the morning – 'pumping and dumping', a tedious but necessary ritual. Because I needed that drink.

Alcohol dulled the overwhelm. It took the edge off the

boredom. By the evening, I wasn't just unwinding, I was reclaiming myself.

At first, it was just a glass in the evening. A small way to press pause on the chaos of motherhood. But here's the thing: when you use alcohol to manage emotions... and those emotions come up daily... then drinking daily becomes dangerously easy. And it did.

One drink in the evening became one as soon as my husband walked through the door. Then, one as soon as I knew he'd left the office and was on his way home.

Because once you believe alcohol is your escape, your reset button, your coping strategy...

It stops being a choice.

THE ESCAPE THAT BECAME A TRAP

Many of us feel deeply uncomfortable sitting in our emotions. It can feel like swimming in murky water – where you're uneasy and unsure about what might be beneath the surface, and you know that movement is bound to stir it up. At certain stages of life, we are simply too depleted to do the work of processing our feelings. So we reach for a quick fix. A shortcut. Something to make the bad feelings go away.

And alcohol? It's the easiest one of all.

It's accessible. It's socially acceptable. It doesn't require an explanation. No one questions a tired mother pouring a glass of wine at the end of the day. Especially if they are unaware of those she's already had in secret.

Of course, alcohol isn't the only thing we use to dodge discomfort. People numb out in all kinds of ways, through work, gambling, social media, over/under-eating, gaming, other drugs. And the reason we cling to these things is because in the short term, they work.

They take away the discomfort. They numb the ache. They provide a fleeting escape.

But they also hook us.

Because these things don't just suppress unwanted emotions; they deliver a burst of pleasure – a momentary high – and as humans, we are wired to run from pain and towards pleasure.

In the end, I had given alcohol so many jobs, so many responsibilities, so much power over my emotional world that I drank heavily every single day.

And that's how I became addicted.

And stuck.

THE STORIES WE TELL OURSELVES

We humans are natural born storytellers. From first cave drawings to modern-day social media, storytelling is how we make sense of the world. It is also how we make sense of ourselves. We tell stories about ourselves all the time. A constant narrative in our heads.

Who we are… and who we're not.

What we are… and what we're not.

Who we can become, what we can never be… and why.

When I coach clients around alcohol, I always remind them of one crucial truth: while alcohol may have become a problem, it was never *the* problem. It's not the root cause, it's an ineffective solution to something deeper.

Most often, that 'something' can be traced back to subconscious beliefs and the stories we've been carrying, often for decades, without even realising it. And we all have them by the way:

1. I'm not smart enough.
2. I'm not attractive enough.
3. I'm not interesting enough.
4. I'm not cool enough.
5. I'm not confident enough.
6. I'm not brave enough.

'A belief is not a fact – it's a fact plus a story' suggests Chris Janssen, Performance & Mindset Coach, and bestselling author of *Grace Yourself: How to Show Up for the Sober Life You Want*.

In other words, 'I screwed up my Oxford exam' is a fact related to that one moment in time, back in 1988. But 'I'm not smart enough' is a story I layered on top, and built into my identity for the subsequent 30 years.

The more we repeat these stories, the more they start to feel like truths. But they're not. They're just narratives we've rehearsed over and over.

Sitting quietly in the subconscious, they go undetected. They don't announce themselves; but they shape the way we see the world, and the way we see ourselves. In other words, they shape our very identity.

We often focus on our behaviour – how much we're drinking, how often. But beneath that are the beliefs quietly steering the ship. And deeper still, beneath the beliefs, lie our unmet needs. The need to feel safe. Seen. Loved. Connected. Validated. Calm.

Which is why alcohol, for many of us, becomes not just a habit – but a way to meet needs we may not even realise we have.

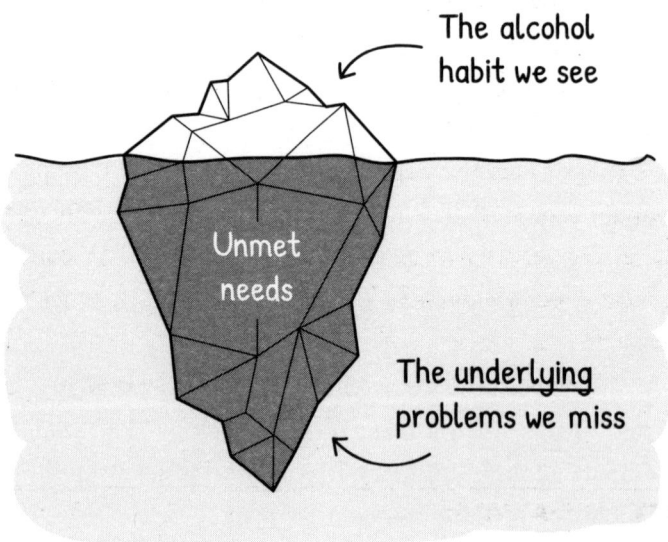

I didn't drink because I walked around consciously thinking 'I'm not smart enough'. That thought never sat front and centre in my mind. But subconsciously I needed to prove to the world that I was. The result? A punishing perfectionism, relentless over-striving, fear of getting it wrong, and a need for validation that set me on a collision course with alcohol. I was constantly falling short, disappointed in myself, exhausted.

Or consider the child that grows up not feeling emotionally seen by a parent.

Their unmet need is to feel seen and valued.

The belief they form is 'I'm not interesting enough'. Or 'I need to perform to be loved'. 'I need to be more entertaining, funnier.'

Their behaviour becomes attention-seeking and over-achieving.

Enter alcohol, to help them feel more confident and expressive.

A drink takes the edge off the self-doubt. It loosens our tongue, makes us feel wittier, more relaxed. It silences the voice that tells us we're a bit dull. Over time, we come to associate alcohol with feeling more like the person we wish we were.

Just like that, we have given alcohol a job to do.

KEY TAKE-AWAYS:

- Alcohol is a functional tool, until it's not. Drinking starts as a choice, then becomes automatic. Small, subconscious choices easily become habits, and those habits can become dependencies without us realising it.

- Alcohol's job description expands over time. What starts as a social lubricant in early adulthood evolves into a stress reliever, a coping mechanism, and even an escape from deeper emotional struggles.
- Alcohol isn't just something we use, it's something we trust. We hand over responsibility for relaxation, confidence, fun, and even our sense of identity to alcohol, often without questioning it.
- Society reinforces the belief that alcohol is essential. From celebrations to commiserations, alcohol is deeply embedded in our culture, making it feel like a default part of life.
- The 'Chief Emotions Officer' problem. Over time, alcohol takes on too many roles in our emotional regulation, leaving us reliant on it to handle stress, anxiety, sadness and self-doubt.

Food for thought:

1. **What jobs have you given alcohol to do in your life?**
   How has its role changed over time and are there any jobs you could manage differently?

2. **What belief sits behind your drinking choices?**
   Do you drink because you want to, or because you believe you need to? Is alcohol truly serving you, or is it just something you've never questioned?

3. **How does alcohol show up in your biggest life moments?**
   Is it part of your celebrations, your stress relief, your social

life, your identity? Could you imagine those moments without it?

4. **Can you recognise a cycle of emotional outsourcing in your life?**
   Do you rely on alcohol (or something else) to handle discomfort? When do you feel most compelled to drink?

5. **Have you ever felt pressure to 'put on a face' that's happier than you really are?**
   How has this influenced your drinking? What would it feel like to fully accept your emotions rather than suppress them?

6. **What role does perfectionism play in your drinking?**
   Do you ever feel like you have to prove yourself in order to be enough? Has drinking ever felt like a release valve from these pressures?

Relevant podcast episodes:

Episode 1. What The Big Drink Rethink is All About
Episode 2. Exploring our Love Affair with Alcohol
Episode 5. The Nation's Favourite Coping Mechanism
Episode 58. Own Your Worth & Rewrite Your Alcohol Story
Episode 62. Our Alcohol Stories: Words that Can Change Your Life

CHAPTER 3

THE BIG SELL

Hang on a minute. How and when did we start believing that alcohol can fulfil our unmet needs? That it can plug these perceived gaps?

Because we don't just wake up one day and decide that alcohol is the key to confidence, validation, love, connection or happiness.

Partly, as we have seen, we tell ourselves stories about ourselves. But we are sold stories too.

In fact we are constantly being conditioned by a hugely powerful story-teller: the marketing industry.

Picture this scene.

A rooftop bar at sunset. The golden light catches the rim of delicate champagne flutes, laughter spills into the warm air, and a group of effortlessly glamorous people are toasting something – success, friendship, the sheer joy of being alive. The women are radiant, all tousled hair, uncreased linen and expensive laughter. The men are charismatic, confident, the kind who seem like they know something about life that you don't.

Then comes the tag line, delivered in a voice as smooth as the drink itself:

'For those who know how to live.'

That's the hook.

Because what if you're not entirely sure that you know how to live?

What if, in fact, life has been feeling a bit messy lately? What if all your hard work still hasn't brought you that job promotion? What if you're beginning to feel like you don't quite measure up? And the secrets of success are feeling a bit elusive?

Now that tagline speaks directly to the doubt and the yearning.

It offers an answer.

And in that moment, the ad isn't just selling champagne. It's selling an identity. It's whispering: 'Drink this, and you'll be more like them'.

More confident. More interesting. More magnetic.

And here's the thing: it works.

WHY YOUR DRINKING ISN'T AN INDEPENDENT CHOICE

As I mentioned in the introduction to this book, before becoming an alcohol mindset coach, I spent 25+ years in advertising. As a Strategist, I worked with brands to convince people to buy their products. It was my job to determine who we were targeting, what problem we needed to position the brand as a solution for, and how to persuade people to choose their product over the competition.

Let me tell you something with absolute certainty: advertising is about much more than merely selling a product. It's an industry built on pre-conditioning your decisions before you even realise you're making them.

Now, you might be thinking: 'Not me. I make my own choices. I'm not swayed by advertising…' Well, I hate to break it to you, but that's exactly why advertising is so powerful.

Thinking you're immune to influence is the greatest misconception of all – and ironically, it's what makes advertising work even better.

The power of alcohol advertising

If you want proof of how powerful alcohol advertising is, simply look at the numbers. The alcohol industry spends eye-watering sums on marketing – nearly £1 billion per year in the UK alone, with global estimates reaching a staggering $1 trillion.

Just let that sink in for a moment.

A trillion-dollar industry dedicated to making sure you keep drinking.

Imagine if a trillion dollars had been spent marketing cocaine last year? The world would be outraged, governments would be in crisis, and public health campaigns would be rolled out overnight.

But because it's alcohol, we don't bat an eyelid.

And that's by design. Over the years, the alcohol industry – alongside policymakers – has carefully positioned alcohol as something different to the other drugs within its class (not just cocaine, but also marijuana and LSD). Something safer. More civilised. More acceptable.

But strip away the branding, the rituals, the cultural gloss, and what you are left with is an addictive and harmful psychoactive substance, masterfully marketed as a lifestyle choice.

Selling a dream, not a drink

To return for a moment to our sun-kissed rooftop bar... The thing that makes alcohol advertising so damn powerful is that brands sell not just a drink in a bottle, but aspirations and illusions. This is common to so many 'lifestyle' categories. For example:

1. Perfume brands don't sell smelly liquid – they sell seduction and allure.
2. Car brands don't sell body panels and engines – they sell freedom and adventure.
3. Sportswear brands don't sell carbon-fibre tennis rackets – they sell guts, attitude and winning.

In fact, the most compelling brand ads say almost nothing about the product itself. Instead, they tap into deep-seated human desires and sell us a fantasy – a pathway to the life we want. Marketers call it the 'higher order benefit', i.e. the elevated, or inflated human desire that they wish to align their brand to.

Hence that tagline: 'For those who know how to live.' Not a thing mentioned about the intrinsic nature of the product, just champagne being aligned with beautiful people and success. Likewise, vodka promises mystery, rebellion, and untouchable coolness; whisky sells wisdom, intelligence, power. Wine brands sell sophistication and class – predominantly to women. Beers are all about belonging, camaraderie and brotherhood.

No one drinks alcohol because they want to consume ethanol mixed with flavouring. They drink because they've been taught to believe it means something about them.

Playing on vulnerabilities

The most powerful advertising of all is the type that speaks to our emotions. Taps into how we feel and, more importantly, how we want to feel. To put it bluntly, advertising exploits vulnerabilities. In the case of alcohol, it tells us that it will do all those 'jobs' mentioned in the previous two chapters. That it will give us what we believe we lack.

- Feeling socially awkward? Have a drink – now you're the life of the party.
- Frazzled at the end of the day? Mix a gin and tonic – have a well-deserved reward.
- Feeling left out? Crack open a beer – now you're one of the lads.

Another psychological lever that alcohol brands can pull is 'social proof'. The notion that 'everyone else is doing it'. In the strategist's toolkit, social norming rules supreme – when you see alcohol everywhere, not just in ads, but through product placements in shows, in films and on TV, at sports events, on social media, etc – it stops being a choice and starts being just the way things are.

Even more insidiously, by inference this ubiquity makes non-drinkers look like the outsiders. The ones missing out. The ones not having fun, while the rest of the world clinks glasses and makes memories.

And if you think this is accidental, think again. In 2009, a House of Commons Health Select Committee investigation gained access to internal marketing documents from alcohol producers and their ad agencies. They found overwhelming evidence that alcohol brands deliberately target young people. That they use gendered messaging to appeal to masculinity and femininity. And that they actively link alcohol with social success. Hundreds of millions of pounds are funnelled into advertising to portray alcohol as the ultimate symbol of coolness, sexiness and achievement.

It is calculated.

It is strategic.

WELCOME TO THE STRATEGY ROOM

I want to invite you into the beating heart of an ad agency, a place where every decision is calculated, and where behaviours are engineered.

Today, the strategy team is working on campaign ideas for a new alcohol account. It all starts with the creative brief – the document that will determine how people think about a brand, when they drink it, why they drink it, and how often they reach for it.

Let's break it down.

1. The objective

Ultimately, this is about one thing – sales. It's about getting a return on investment (ROI), which means that every £1 spent on advertising must generate £4, £5, even £6 in sales. This is why we can say with absolute certainty that alcohol advertising works, because brands wouldn't invest around a trillion dollars a year globally on marketing if it didn't pay back in profits multiple times over.

In order to generate these kinds of returns, they tend to focus on three key areas:

a) *Growing the market by hooking new drinkers in – preferably young ones.* The alcohol industry knows that long-term profits depend on bringing new drinkers into the fold, and the younger, the better. The goal is to normalise drinking early, subtly planting the idea that alcohol is essential to social success, fun and coming of age. The earlier young people see alcohol advertising, the more likely they are to drink and to drink heavily. As far as the industry is concerned, it's get them in early and keep them loyal. 'Customers for life' are of phenomenally high cumulative value.

Take Aperol, for instance. Once a little-known, unfashionable, Italian aperitif, it quietly repositioned itself as the drink of summer for millennials – light, breezy and effortlessly Instagrammable. The reinvention targeted a generation motivated by experiences, aesthetics and shareability. It wasn't just about taste any more. It was about terraces in Tuscany, sunlit laughter and a kind of curated spontaneity that looked perfect through an orange-tinted filter. Through vibrant ads, music festival sponsorships and 'Spritz Socials' designed for maximum social media kudos, Aperol didn't just sell a drink – it sold a lifestyle. And it worked. According to the magazine, *The Grocer*, Aperol's UK sales surged by 42% in the two years following the repositioning.

b) *Increasing the frequency of consumption*, i.e. get current drinkers to drink more often. This is one of the easiest ways to increase revenue, because customers are already consumers, already parti pris as it were, so the role of marketing is simply to present the brand as being relevant to additional drinking occasions.

For instance, the phrase 'Perfect with nibbles' quietly reframes alcohol as part of a snack routine, not just a celebratory event. Similarly, 'A great way to unwind after work' isn't just a suggestion – it's a narrative that normalises alcohol as the default coping mechanism for stress, implying that drinking is not indulgent, but deserved.

Famously, Pimms used the tagline 'It's Pimm's o'clock' to create an occasion where none previously existed. Instead of waiting for a summer party or Wimbledon, the brand gave consumers permission to drink 'whenever' – turning time itself into a reason.

The phrase mimics the cultural rhythm of 'It's 5 o'clock somewhere', linking alcohol to moments, moods and markers of the day. Once a brand owns an occasion – whether it's 'aperitivo hour', 'bottomless brunch' or 'Pimm's o'clock' – it inserts itself into people's internal calendars, much like coffee after lunch or tea before bed.

It's a masterstroke of behavioural design: reduce the friction of decision-making, create a socially endorsed cue, and align your product with an emotional reward (relaxation, pleasure, belonging).

c) *Encouraging 'switching', i.e. stealing customers from competitors.* So, alcohol marketing isn't just about getting you to drink more – it's also about getting you to drink *theirs*. The goal here is to tempt consumers away from competitor brands by creating sharper, more emotionally resonant identities.

Take Heineken, for example. Their multimillion-pound sponsorships of major sporting events – from the UEFA Champions League to Formula 1 – are not just about visibility. They're a deliberate attempt to own a moment, a mood, and a tribe. If you're already a Carlsberg drinker, Heineken doesn't need to convince you to drink beer – they just need to persuade you that theirs is the brand for real fans. The more they align themselves with elite sport, camaraderie and global cool, the more likely you are to question whether your current choice measures up.

Anyway, back to our fictitious creative brief: let's imagine we're doing one for pink gin – i.e. we want 'to make gin, which has historically appealed more to men, resonate with female drinkers. In doing this we aim to open up a whole new audience and extend sales by £X million per year.'

First, we need to define our target audience.

2. Who are we targeting?

This is where we create a 'pen portrait' of the drinker we want to convert – beyond basic demographics (age, income, gender), we establish who they are, who they aspire to be, and what they struggle with. It's where marketing stops being about alcohol and starts being about identity.

So in creating a campaign for a gin brand that targets women, we don't just ask: 'Which women drink gin?', we ask:

- Which women don't drink gin yet, but could?
- What's stopping them?
- How do we make gin the answer to something they want, or the conduit to the experiences they want or the person they want to be?

Let's add a pen portrait to our brief:

> *'Our target audience is women in their late 20s to mid-40s who feel alienated by traditional spirits advertising. They don't see themselves reflected in whisky ads, which feel too masculine, or in rum ads, which feel too rebellious. They love the social nature of wine but are looking for something new – something*

more fun, creative, modern, and effortlessly cool.'

There's one thing missing here: we haven't yet tapped into their vulnerabilities. Most purchases are made with the heart, not the head, so the feelings that the brand evokes are a vital part of the brief.

3. What do we want them to think and feel?

Remember, alcohol marketing never sells alcohol. It sells an emotional 'hook':

- Status.
- Confidence.
- Social belonging.
- Sex appeal.
- Escape.

We don't want our target female audience to just drink the gin. We want them to see gin as part of their identity. For it to speak of who they are, and the kind of choices they make in life. It needs to stand for how they wish to be seen (e.g. popular, cutting edge, stylish and spontaneous), and it needs to align with what they value (e.g. spontaneity, friendship, connection and positivity).

So for our example creative brief, the brand positioning statement would be:

'X Gin is not just a drink – it's a mindset. It's for women who want to enhance their every day experience, who

crave something more sophisticated than beer and more exciting than wine. This is not a spirit for special occasions – it's the new go-to, the essential drink for a stylish, modern woman on any night spent with friends.'

Cue an ad that shows women laughing at a rooftop bar, glasses clinking, the city lights twinkling. With a caption that reads: 'Here's to the nights you'll never forget, and the stories you'll never tell.'

No mention of botanicals. No mention of distillation. Just emotion, energy, aspiration.

And just like that, we've created desire.

Oh, and let's make it pink. Which is one of the simplest, and arguably most patronising tactics in alcohol marketing.

'MUMMY WINE'

I had the opportunity to talk to Professor Carol Emslie on the podcast. Carol is co-director of the Research Centre for Health at Glasgow Caledonian University and co-chair of the Scottish Alcohol Research Network, and is internationally renowned for her work on gender and alcohol.

Through years of research, she's seen how alcohol is marketed to women as a source of empowerment, friendship, self-care and escape. 'Slim' wine bottles and slogans like 'bra off, hair up, wine poured' are designed to align alcohol with emotional needs – especially among mothers and young women.

Crazily, even moments meant for collective progress, like International Women's Day, are hijacked with hashtags and hollow promises, as brands attempt to affiliate themselves to 'social causes'. That's why we see such initiatives as Johnny Walker launching 'Jane Walker' to celebrate International Women's Day, or Smirnoff teaming up with Spotify to highlight gender imbalances in music.

A few years ago, Carol launched a campaign against the feminisation of alcohol called 'Don't Pink My Drink' to expose these tactics for what they are: cynical, calculated and harmful. 'Pink prosecco, pink gin, pink craft gin, pink lemonade with vodka. Just make it pink. Think pink, drink pink, pretty in pink, pink up your picnic, pink your drink...' It's obvious, it's lazy, but it works – the industry knows that if they bathe or package their product in pastel tones, women will buy it.

As Carol points out, this gendered playbook is lifted straight from the tobacco industry, which years ago, pushed 'feminine' cigarette brands like Virginia Slims with the tagline: 'You've come a long way, baby.'

In this ever-evolving landscape, alcohol companies are raising the bar in their efforts to craft narratives around their products that resonate with women. The idea of a glass of 'mummy wine' to unwind at the end of a long day, for example, to cope with the feeling of isolation and the overwhelm of responsibility, is a direct strategy to target new mothers at a vulnerable and stressful time of their lives.

Never have pink drinks been so accessible – single-serve wine drinks and ready-mixed spirits and cocktails are currently the fastest-growing section of the alcohol market, and are a masterclass in how to create a sense of need where you didn't know you even had one. 'Just the one', they whisper. 'Come on, you don't even have to pour it into a glass – it will slip easily into your handbag and you can have it on the go.'

THE BITS THAT ALCOHOL ADS NEVER TELL YOU

The crazy thing is that despite the scale of its influence, alcohol advertising operates in a world free from real accountability. Unlike other potentially harmful substances, the alcohol industry isn't required to be honest about its risks. There are no regulations that demand that alcohol ads mention that:

1. Alcohol is addictive.
2. It has no nutritional value, but is high in sugar and calories.
3. It has proven links to a great many diseases and health issues.
4. It dulls your senses and increases the risk of finding yourself in dangerous and vulnerable situations.

If alcohol were a food, it would be slapped with all manner of labelling protocols and warnings. Indeed, if alcohol didn't already exist, and a company tried to launch it as a brand-new product today, they'd stand no chance of ever getting it to market.

This was a point of view reinforced by Professor David Nutt when he appeared on my podcast: 'If alcohol were invented today and submitted for approval, it would fail. No question. It is a substance with well-documented links to cancer, liver disease, mental health disorders, addiction and fatal accidents.

Any new drink that caused the same level of harm as alcohol does daily would be banned immediately. But because alcohol has been culturally normalised, these risks are ignored, hidden in plain sight.'

YOU'RE ON YOUR OWN

No one is protecting us from the harms of alcohol – not really. We certainly can't expect the alcohol industry to push for tighter regulation. Why would it? Its goal isn't to protect our health – it's to keep us drinking. To keep us hooked.

And the government? It's not stepping in either. Because while alcohol causes untold damage to our society, it's also big business. The Treasury earns billions from it every year. Regulating it too heavily would hit their bottom line hard, and immediately.

In the UK, alcohol marketing is largely self- and co-regulated. The very companies that profit from alcohol consumption are allowed to help decide how it's advertised, packaged and promoted. TV and radio ads fall under 'co-regulation' between Ofcom and the Advertising Standards Authority – an industry-funded body. Packaging and sponsorship, meanwhile, are governed by the Portman Group, an organisation set up and funded by the alcohol industry itself. Critics, including public health groups, frequently point out this conflict of interest, and have called for stronger, statutory regulation.

And so, despite increasing growing concern about youth exposure and rising support for tighter regulation, alcohol marketing is still everywhere – woven into the fabric of our daily lives and openly targeted at the next generation. Let's be clear, alcohol brands aren't just selling to us – they're selling to our children via the likes of sponsorship of football tournaments and music festivals, product placement in TV shows and blockbuster films, ads in social media feeds, celebrity endorsements and all the endless eye-catching promotions in supermarkets and corner shops.

And while the profits stack up, the rest of us are left to pick up the tab.

In 2023/24, the UK government made £12.5 billion from alcohol duties. But the cost of alcohol harm in England alone? An estimated £27.4 billion a year. That includes £4.9 billion on healthcare, £14.6 billion on crime and policing, £5 billion in lost productivity (e.g. absenteeism), and £2.9 billion on social services.

Go figure.

KEY TAKE-AWAYS

- Alcohol advertising doesn't just sell a drink – it sells an identity.
- Alcohol brands use psychological levers to hook new drinkers and increase consumption.
- Gendered marketing targets women through stereotypes, empowerment messaging and 'pinkifying' products.
- Alcohol companies align with social causes to appear progressive while selling a product that carries real risks.
- Government regulation is weak because alcohol generates billions in tax revenue, making it politically difficult to restrict.
- If alcohol were invented today, it wouldn't pass health or safety standards. But because it's always been here, it gets a cultural free pass.

Food for thought:

1. **How much of your drinking is truly your choice?**
   Have you ever questioned why you drink, or do you just assume it's 'normal'?

2. **What emotions or identities do you associate with alcohol, and where did those beliefs come from?**
   Do you drink because you think it makes you more fun, confident, or social? When did you first learn to connect alcohol with these feelings?

3. **Have you been influenced by alcohol marketing without realising it?**

Have you ever been drawn to a drink because it felt like it was 'for people like me'? How often do you see alcohol linked to female empowerment, bonding or self-care?

4. **How much of this marketing do you unconsciously absorb every day?**
Keep an eye out, and see if you go a full day without seeing an alcohol ad, product placement, or branded sponsorship. What effect might this constant exposure be having on your perception of drinking?

5. **If alcohol were invented today, would you still feel the same way about it?**
If alcohol came with the same health warnings as cigarettes or hard drugs, would you drink it?

Related podcast episodes:
Episode 2. Exploring our Love Affair With Alcohol
Episode 33. Alcohol Advertising: It's Time for a Rethink
Episode 51. The Hidden Cost of Alcohol – A Police Perspective
Episode 60. The Gendered World of Alcohol Marketing

CHAPTER 4

THE TROUBLE WITH SWISS ARMY KNIVES

The Swiss Army Knife was originally developed by the Swiss company Victorinox in the late 19th century, and rapidly became symbolic of usefulness and reliability. Known for its compact design and portability, it is a multi-functional tool, always there for emergencies and everyday tasks. It typically includes a variety of tools, such as:

- Knife blade: a sharp blade for cutting.
- Screwdriver: a flathead or Phillips head screwdriver for tightening or loosening screws.
- Bottle opener: for opening bottles with caps.
- Can opener: for opening tin cans.
- Scissors: for cutting small items.
- Tweezers: for precision tasks, like removing splinters.
- Toothpick: for personal hygiene.
- Corkscrew: for opening wine bottles.
- File: for filing rough edges.

Some models include additional features like saws, magnifying glasses, pliers, or even, nowadays, digital tools such as USB drives or LED lights.

I tend to think of alcohol as a Swiss Army Knife for life's challenges. It's a tool that's always within reach and that we turn to for many purposes. Much like the famous Swiss multi-tool, it promises versatility: a drink for every occasion, a solution for every mood.

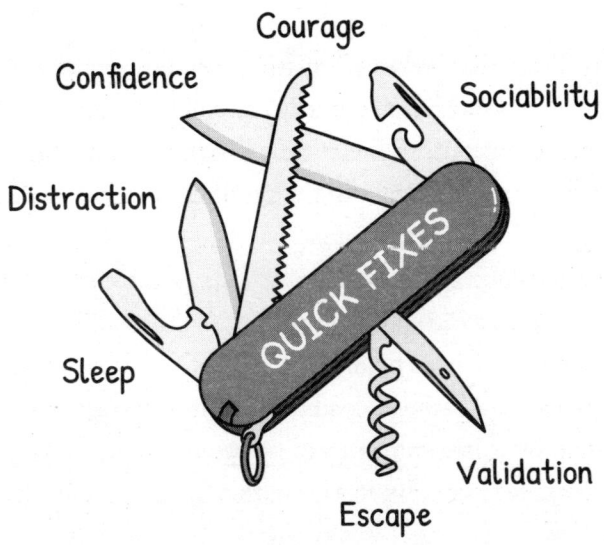

But the trouble with Swiss Army Knives is that ultimately they offer a quick fix.

And while they can do a lot, they don't excel at any one thing. They give the illusion of utility. The tiny scissors can't match the precision of proper shears, the screwdriver struggles with anything beyond a minor fix, and the blade? Fine for small jobs but no substitute for a proper chef's knife. In other words, when you want to do something properly – it's a bit shit (apart for the bottle opener, ironically – that's actually pretty good).

OUR QUICK-FIX SOCIETY

As a society, we've been sold the idea that there's a shortcut for everything – stress? Grab a drink. Exhausted? Another coffee. Feeling low? Retail therapy or a scroll through social media will sort it out. The relentless pace of modern life has amplified our craving for instant gratification. We've been trained to expect everything *now!*

It's not our fault. When our to-do lists never seem to end and the pressure to 'keep up' is constant, who has time to dig deep when there's always another email to answer, another meeting to attend, another load of laundry waiting?

The trouble is, these band-aid solutions often mask the problem rather than solve it. While they promise relief, they rarely satisfy us for long. Instead, they keep us stuck in a cycle of chasing the next hit, never quite addressing what we truly need.

The good news is that we have the power to rethink this cycle. What if, instead, we found small ways to pause and truly care for ourselves, even amidst the busyness? It might just be the reset we've been craving.

THE WAY ALCOHOL WORKS

Alcohol is both a stimulant and a depressant. Its effects on the brain can temporarily dull emotional pain, quiet overactive thoughts, and create a sense of relaxation or euphoria. In social settings, it can act as a fast-track to confidence, lowering inhibitions and making interactions feel smoother.

However, this quick fix is deeply deceptive. Alcohol doesn't flood the brain with dopamine like some drugs (e.g. cocaine), it inhibits the GABA neurons that normally suppress dopamine activity. So by silencing the brakes (inhibitory neurons), alcohol allows more dopamine to be released. That's what creates the initial buzz or mild euphoria.

There is nothing wrong with dopamine, by the way. In fact, it's a lovely thing. It's key to our being able to repeat pleasurable experiences. Also known as the 'reward chemical', it instructs the brain to remember what has stimulated it, because it will want to repeat the feeling. Unfortunately, though, drinking alcohol leads to *artificial* stimulation of dopamine – in quantities that kick off an imbalanced chain reaction.

When alcohol enters our bloodstream, our blood alcohol content rises (our BAC), along with the dopamine, but this pleasurable lift only lasts for about 20–30 minutes – because in response to this artificial input of dopamine, the brain, in its quest for balance, produces a counter-chemical called dynorphin. Dynorphin is a depressant with sedative effects. It brings our mood down, and lingers for longer than dopamine – up to three to four hours – taking our mood lower than it was before we started drinking.

This physiological, chemical and biological response to alcohol is universal. No one is immune. The degree of 'up' and the length of time this lasts and the degree of 'down' and the lingering effects will vary from person to person, but it's a roller-coaster ride we all end up on.

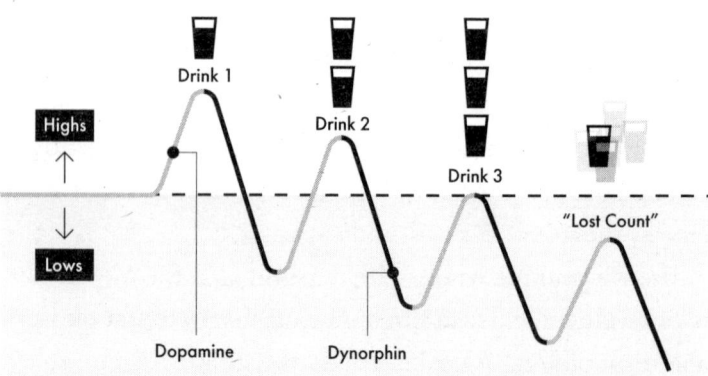

As our mood dips, our brain remembers where the initial high came from and urges us to repeat what we did to get that dopamine, i.e. have another drink. This is why we find it so hard to stop at one. And the more we drink, the lower our mood becomes (because of the dynorphin), and try as we might, with each successive glass, we can't rekindle the levels of positivity we were at before the first one.

Therefore, ironically, handing alcohol the job of enhancing our mood, is not only a quick fix with a 20–30-minute ceiling, it's a guaranteed route to feeling worse thereafter. It's basically why we can get very emotional, teary and sentimental at the end of an evening.

And it doesn't stop there.

The chemical 'chain reaction' set in motion by drinking alcohol also stimulates the adrenal gland, which is responsible for the production of adrenalin and cortisol. These stress hormones, which flood the system and peak after your last drink, are the reason behind the middle-of-the-night heart-racing and deep panic and anxiety that many of us experience. Unpleasant feelings that again linger way longer than any initial mood lift, often lasting into the next day as the 'booze blues' or 'hangxiety'.

Nick Elston, renowned speaker and mental health advocate, described how for him alcohol was a 'release valve'. A quick way to let off steam at the end of a hard day. But the more he relied on it, the more he saw the illusion – alcohol wasn't resolving anything, just pressing 'pause' on his anxiety before amplifying it the next day.

The solution became the cause, and the only way to escape was to keep drinking. So, the vicious cycle continued.

When William Porter, author of *Alcohol Explained*, came on to the podcast, this is how he described the turbulence that alcohol creates in our brains: 'The human brain creates and excretes its own array of chemicals, drugs and hormones. It's a very complicated process that we don't fully understand, but what we do know is it works by something called homeostasis – which is the ideal balance of all these chemicals, drugs and hormones. They wake you up, they put you to sleep, they make you feel happy, sad, excited, whatever it is, and your brain is constantly trying to keep things in balance – which it generally manages to do.

'Now, when you introduce something like alcohol, your brain senses a disturbance to that balance and it tries to counter it. And it does it in lots of different ways, one of which is to produce more adrenaline and cortisol, which is a stress hormone that counters the sedating effects of the alcohol. But when the alcohol wears off, that over-sensitisation – that extra stress that the body has created to counter the sedating effect of the alcohol – remains. And this creates a feeling of being uptight and anxious.'

When I was a heavy drinker, I experienced those manic episodes on a nightly basis. A cyclical 3.30–5am insomnia during which every negative, catastrophic thought in my head would ricochet around and create panic. Hideous. Just awful. Without knowing all of the above – everything that was going on in my brain and my body – I didn't realise those enduring lows were the long tail effect of alcohol - and the very reason why I would ultimately want to drink again the next day. And yet perhaps it should have been obvious: because whilst alcohol had created the chemical reaction responsible for throwing my brain chemistry out of whack, it was now the quickest way to fix it. So drinking the next day/evening became an inevitability, as I went in search of the 'sedative' to deal with the stress and anxiety IT had created.

The way William Porter explained it made a lot of sense to me: 'I liken it to a memory foam mattresses,' he said. 'They're quite hard when you first lie down, but you slowly sink into them, so that when you get up, there's like a "you-shaped" indent in the bed. That's basically what happens in your brain when you drink. You are imprinting the memory of that drink on your brain. And then, when you stop drinking, there's a hole there. I realised this when I woke up feeling horrible each morning, until of course the next drink would fill that hole and make me feel better. But, and I suppose this is the key… it was never making me feel better than if I had never drunk – and created that hole – in the first place.'

In other words, *alcohol can only ever give back what it's taken in the first place.*

Think about that… I'm going to say it again and urge you to look back at the direction of travel described above. *Alcohol can only ever give back what it's taken in the first place.*

So it's not just the ultimate quick fix, but the instigator of a dangerous cycle of quick fixes, one which can fast-track alcohol's promotion from PA to CEO.

At this point, William picked up the analogy of the Swiss Army Knife and ran with it. 'It's a very good way of looking at alcohol, but I am imagining it left lying around with all the blades open, so that when you pick it up, you cut yourself. Where whatever good you think it's doing, it's actually doing you more harm. You may get the stone out of the shoe, but your hands are all cut to pieces in the process.'

It should be said that of course these loops aren't always dramatic or destructive. Sometimes, they're quiet – just enough to keep you tired, stressed, or slightly off balance, without ever raising a red flag.

But the unfortunate truth is that in pretty much any instance where you use alcohol to do a job, it creates bigger issues that compel ongoing use. In other words, it creates a world of ever-increasing vicious cycles.

vicious cycle
[noun s.]
A chain of events in which the response to one difficulty creates a new problem that aggravates the original difficulty
(Source: Merriam-Webster)

Alcohol and mental health
About one in four people in the UK will experience a mental health problem each year.

The relationship between alcohol and mental health is complex, but given the emotional 'rollercoaster' triggered by drinking – the way alcohol alters our brain chemistry and floods our system with stress hormones – we can clearly see that the links are there.

And yet… alcohol has been described by the UK Medical Council as the 'nation's favourite coping mechanism', with many of us drinking to try to help manage stress, anxiety, depression or other mental health problems.

Drinking to cope is self-medication – and you don't need to be in crisis to be doing it. Many people use alcohol to take the edge off a long day without even realising they're outsourcing emotional regulation. Unlike all formal medications, however, this one doesn't come with a neatly folded leaflet identifying the risks, contra-indications and potential side-effects. If it did, it might read:

- Temporary relief followed by increased anxiety, disrupted brain chemistry and emotional instability.

- Significantly increases risk of depression, emotional dysregulation and long-term mental health decline.
- May cause dependency, worsening the very symptoms it promises to relieve – notably low mood, anxiety and depression.

Depression and heavy drinking have a mutually reinforcing relationship – meaning that either condition increases a person's chances of experiencing the other:

Feel low > drink to escape > alcohol increases depressive symptoms > drink more to cope > deeper depression.

And so it is that people struggling with depression are more likely to drink heavily; and people who drink heavily are more likely to develop depression.

The true cost of self-medicating with alcohol is that we're not actually addressing the problem. We're avoiding it. It's like slapping a bandage on a deep wound without ever cleaning it.

Alcohol papers over the cracks, but those cracks don't go away. They grow into fault lines beneath the surface, increasingly threatening our emotional well-being as the real issues go unaddressed.

And the more we rely on alcohol to cope, the harder it becomes to imagine handling life without it.

But here's the truth: if alcohol was the answer, mental health wouldn't be in crisis.

Alcohol and sleep

Sleep is such an important part of our wellbeing, and many of us believe that alcohol helps us sleep. That it helps us relax and wind down at the end of a stressful day before we climb into bed.

But the truth is that alcohol doesn't put you to sleep. It knocks you out.

And being unconscious is not the same as sleeping.

Neuroscientist Matthew Walker, author of *Why We Sleep*, doesn't even call what happens after drinking 'sleep'. Instead, he refers to it as 'alcohol-induced unconsciousness'.

Because that's what it is; a chemically induced shutdown, not natural, restorative rest.

And that distinction really, REALLY matters.

Because sleep isn't just about lying down for eight hours. It's about what happens during those hours: the intricate, vital processes that keep us emotionally stable, mentally sharp and physically well. It's about cycles, and in simple terms:

- Deep sleep repairs the body.
- REM sleep restores the mind.

Alcohol disrupts the natural flow and depth of these cycles.

Deep sleep (slow-wave sleep) may initially increase in the first half of the night (because alcohol sedates you), but it's often shallow and fragmented. Whilst REM sleep gets heavily suppressed, especially in the second half of the night when alcohol is being metabolised – this is when vivid dreaming, emotional processing and memory consolidation usually happen. On top of this, fragmented sleep causes repeated wake-ups – whether you remember them or not. The truth is that, while a drink might feel like it helps you unwind, it robs you of the very rest your brain and body need most.

So even if your Fitbit, Oura ring or Apple watch shows some deep or REM sleep, the structure, intensity and timing are likely off. These wearable devices are great at tracking sleep patterns (movement, heart rate, maybe even temperature), but they can't directly measure brain activity. The only way to truly assess deep or REM sleep is through polysomnography (a sleep lab test with EEG monitoring). So your ring might say 'you got 20% REM', but it can't tell how restorative that REM actually was.

When your brain's natural sleep rhythm is fundamentally disrupted in this way, it leaves you feeling groggy and depleted the next day. Alcohol may seem to help you drift off, but it leaves you more exhausted, more anxious and therefore more dependent on it to sleep the next night. As William Porter phrased it: 'Drinking before bed is like taking a hammer to your mental health.'

It's yet another vicious cycle: alcohol keeps you permanently running on empty. As William explained: 'When you drink regularly, the alcohol never really leaves your system. It has a half-life of five hours, meaning even if you stop at 10pm, it's still affecting your sleep long into the night. The brain is constantly compensating, leaving you in a state of chemical imbalance. And so you wake up feeling drained, sluggish and fragile. You haven't had real sleep. You've had a chemically disrupted cycle that has robbed you of rest.'

And it doesn't matter whether you're drinking heavily, as I was, or if you're just having one or two, because even one or two drinks seriously interrupts your ability to go into those natural sleep cycles.

A study cited by Hackensack Meridian Health found that:

- A small serving of alcohol (under two drinks for men and under one for women) can decrease sleep quality by 9.3%.
- A moderate serving (about two drinks for men and one for women) can decrease sleep quality by 24%.
- A large serving (more than two drinks for men and more than one for women) can decrease sleep quality by 39.2%.

Additionally, a survey reported by the Sleep Foundation indicated that about 40% of respondents noticed a significant impact on their sleep after consuming three to four drinks.

THE PARENT TRAP

There ain't no doubt about it, parenthood is exhausting. Physically, mentally and emotionally exhausting. Nothing that comes before in life can prepare you for the reality of raising tiny humans. It hit me like a tidal wave.

It's a level of depletion you can't fully grasp until you're in it, so it's no surprise that so many parents turn to alcohol, as I sure did, as a coping mechanism.

At the end of the day, when the kids are finally asleep and the house is quiet, that glass of wine or bottle of beer feels like a tiny act of rebellion – a stolen moment of peace in a life that suddenly feels dictated by everyone else's needs.

I remember those evenings so well. Standing in the kitchen, feeling completely frazzled, praying that the kids would sleep through, pouring a glass of wine like it was my hard-earned reward. The unspoken contract I made with myself was simple: 'I got through another day. I deserve this.'

I'm a pretty well-educated woman, but I simply didn't realise at the time that the very thing I was using to 'cope' was actually making me more exhausted, more anxious, and less capable of handling the demands of motherhood. That alcohol was massively contributing to the stresses that drove me to drink. And that my nightly bottle of wine was sabotaging the sleep I needed. Because you know what? Even if the kids did sleep through…. I didn't.

Drinking to cope → ruining sleep → struggling to cope again. A loop so subtle that most of us don't even see it happening.

Every morning, I'd wake up already in survival mode. Already counting down the hours until bedtime so I could have my moment of escape again. Never refreshed. Never restored. Just running on fumes, trying to pour from an empty cup, wondering why everything felt so bloody hard.

And the cruellest part? I blamed myself.

I assumed the exhaustion and the emotional strain was just part of motherhood, and that I was particularly exhausted because I wasn't good at being a mum. Remember my limiting belief? Yet more reinforcement.

THE MENOPAUSE TRAP

If you're female and in your 40s or 50s, the chances are you're not just navigating the pressures of work, parenting and modern life – you may also be moving through one of the biggest hormonal transitions of your life.

Menopause – and the perimenopausal years leading up to it – is a time of huge internal flux. Oestrogen, progesterone and testosterone levels begin to decline, and with them come changes to everything from mood, metabolism, sleep and skin to memory, digestion and emotional regulation.

As menopause expert, Lauren Chiren, explained to me on The Big Drink Rethink, this is a major life stage that affects around 13 million women in the UK at any one time. That's roughly one-third of the entire female population. And yet, staggeringly, 86% of women still say they don't fully understand what menopause is, or how it might impact them.

Unsurprisingly, many women, looking for some respite from this hormonal whirlwind, turn to alcohol. And yet, as a coping mechanism for the symptoms of menopause – anxiety, sleep disruption, low mood, brain fog, joint pain and emotional overwhelm – alcohol couldn't be worse.

As Lauren described it, introducing alcohol into an already-sensitive system is like lobbing a grenade into a room that's already on fire. It disrupts blood sugar levels, amplifies mood swings, contributes to inflammation, interferes with already-fragile sleep cycles, and throws the body's endocrine system – our finely tuned hormone-regulating network – into further chaos.

Ailsa Hichens – author, therapist, and another guest on the podcast – shared how, for years, she misread her menopause symptoms as signs of something darker. The exhaustion. The crying spells. The sense that her confidence had disappeared, almost overnight. She thought she was having a breakdown. Thought she was losing her mind. And like so many women, she reached for the one thing that promised quick relief: a drink.

I remember saying to her: 'It's so hard to know where one thing ends and the next begins.' We both agreed – when alcohol is part of the picture, it muddies the waters. It becomes almost impossible to tell which symptoms are hormonal, and which are alcohol-fuelled. Because so many of them overlap. And so the drink that we're convinced is helping us cope is often the thing intensifying our suffering.

Lauren sees this loop all the time in her work supporting high-functioning women through midlife. Many come to her saying: 'I'll do anything… just don't take away my glass of wine.' It's the one thing they feel they still have control over. But through gentle experiments – cutting back glass by glass, increasing hydration, shifting to unprocessed foods – they start to notice something. Less bloating. Better sleep.

Calmer moods. Fewer aches. More joy.

Not perfect, not easy – but better.

LETTING GO OF THE LIFE RAFT

We are conditioned to believe alcohol is our reward, our right, our relief. For so long, I thought drinking made life 'more' – more fun, more manageable, more bearable. It was my crutch, my reward. I couldn't imagine life without it, because that felt like a 'lesser' life – a mundane, wired and deprived version of the one I knew.

But the truth? There is no drink in the world worth the sleep, energy and peace it robs you of.

When I finally stopped drinking and experienced what it's like to be fully rested, fully present, and actually capable of handling life without alcohol, I realised I had been living a half-life.

Nick Elston described his moment of clarity when he stopped self-medicating with alcohol: 'I always thought I needed alcohol to take the edge off – to bring me peace. But when I finally let go, I realised peace had been there all along. I was just drowning it out.' And that's the recurring reality – alcohol convinces us it's adding something to our lives, but more often than not, it's taking away the very things we're searching for.

William encapsulated this paradox brilliantly at the end of our podcast conversation: 'I kind of thought alcohol was my life raft. And I was clinging onto this raft in this really tumultuous sea, getting tossed around everywhere. And the thought of stopping was like being asked to jettison this life raft which is incredibly scary. But what I found was that when I actually did jettison it, I was actually only standing in two foot of water and I'd had no need of it in the first place.'

But you don't need to go all in to feel the difference. Even small breaks or gentle cutbacks can show you something powerful. You start to see how even one or two drinks can cloud your sleep, dull your energy, or shift your mood in ways you'd simply accepted as normal. And bit by bit, you may realise that the life raft you've been clinging to might not be keeping you afloat – it might be what's weighing you down.

KEY TAKE-AWAYS:

- Alcohol is a Swiss Army Knife for life's challenges, but like all multi-tools, it's a poor substitute for the right tool. It offers quick fixes, but never truly solves the problem.
- In a culture obsessed with instant fixes, alcohol fits the bill, but at a cost. The buzz is borrowed. What it gives, it quickly takes back – often leaving you more anxious, tired and low than before.
- Far from soothing stress, alcohol fuels the very cycles it promises to break. It disrupts sleep, depletes energy, and triggers a biochemical backlash that amplifies panic, low mood and 'hangxiety'.
- Many of us are self-medicating without realising it. What feels like coping is often just being numbed – a pattern that

keeps our deeper needs unmet and emotional resilience undeveloped.
- You don't have to quit completely to see the truth. Even a short break or mindful reset can show you the real impact of drinking – and whether it's truly helping or holding you back.
- Life without alcohol isn't less – it's more. More presence, more patience, more clarity, more calm. When you remove the fog, you can finally see what's possible.

Food for thought:

1. **If alcohol came with a warning label, would you still reach for it?**
   If every bottle listed side effects like anxiety, poor sleep, or mood swings – would it still feel like the shortcut to relaxation?

2. **Do you drink to cope with stress or anxiety, and if so what happens when the effects wear off?**
   Are you soothing the source of your discomfort, or simply delaying its return?

3. **What might alcohol be quietly taking from you?**
   Even if it doesn't feel like a 'problem', could it be draining your energy, dulling your joy, of distancing you from your goals?

4. **What vicious cycles might alcohol be keeping you stuck in?**
   Think about your sleep, mood, motivation or resilience.

Is alcohol solving the problem – or quietly sustaining it?

5. Have you ever mistaken alcohol for a 'life raft'?
Does drinking make you feel safe, comfortable or normal?

6. Have you ever tried changing your drinking?
Not because you had to, but just to see how you'd feel?

Relevant podcast episodes:
Episode 5. The Nation's Favourite Coping Mechanism
Episode 9. The Truth About Alcohol & Sleep
Episode 18. Beyond the Bottle: Nick Elston on Mental Health
Episode 19. Alcohol-free Peace: Self-love, ADHD & Perimenopause
Episode 42. Alcohol & Menopause
Episode 69. Mummy Doesn't Need Wine

CHAPTER 5

HABIT, DEPENDENCY & THE GREY AREA IN-BETWEEN

So far, we've explored the stories we tell ourselves about alcohol – what it promises, what it delivers and where it often falls short. But before we go deeper into the emotional dynamics behind our drinking decisions – and start questioning some of the bigger myths we've been sold – let's pause and talk plainly about behavioural patterns. Because most of us have got them when it comes to alcohol, and if you're reading this, there's a good chance you're not totally at peace with yours.

THE SPACE WHERE MOST OF US LIVE

In my coaching work, I come across a great many people who are starting to question their drinking – not because they've hit a crisis point, but because they're quietly wondering: is this really working for me?

They're not hiding bottles. They're not drinking in the morning. They may be outwardly high-functioning – juggling careers, families, friendships. And yet… they feel flat. Tired.

Frustrated by the gap between who they are and who they want to be. Their drinking isn't dramatic, but it's also not... nothing. They might not drink every day, but they think about it most days. They might not black out, but they regret more than they'd like to admit.

US sobriety coach Jolene Park gave this experience a name: grey area drinking – a term that's resonated with thousands. It describes people who don't fit the stereotype of what we've traditionally seen as a 'problem drinker', but who aren't entirely comfortable either.

This is the murky middle ground. The blurred lines. The space where alcohol hasn't wrecked your life – but it might just be dimming it.

Many people hesitate to look too closely at their drinking because they fear what they'll find. There's a concern that if they acknowledge an issue, it means they will have to take immediate, drastic action. And what if they're not ready? What if they fail to make the change?

But here's the truth: there is no failing this inquiry. There is only awareness. And awareness doesn't force change; it creates choice. The more clearly you understand your drinking, the more control you have over your decisions.

You don't have to change anything right now. You don't have to decide what to do next. You're not committing to anything by simply looking.

This chapter is about understanding your drinking patterns without fear – from a place of curiosity. Because when you get curious, you get clarity. The most freeing thing you can do is to be honest with yourself.

Fifty shades of grey

Most people think of drinking in binary, black-and-white terms: you're either an alcoholic, or you're fine. You are either in real trouble, or there's nothing to worry about.

But the truth is, many drinkers don't fit neatly into either extreme. Instead, they live in the murky in-between – the space where alcohol isn't destroying their life, but it's not exactly serving it either.

And it's this in-between place that so often creates ambivalence. It offers just enough plausible deniability to keep your conscience quiet: I'm not that bad... I can stop anytime... Everyone else drinks too. The ambivalence becomes a kind of emotional camouflage – a way to avoid discomfort without addressing the truth.

And when millions of people live in that same lingering uncertainty, it becomes a cultural blind spot. Society normalises over-drinking and shrugs off the consequences of drinking that isn't 'bad enough'. But the cumulative impact of slightly too much alcohol – on sleep, productivity, self-esteem, relationships, mental health – is huge. The grey area may not scream for attention or even be visible from the outside, but it quietly shapes how we feel, how we show up – and who we become.

Grey area drinkers don't wake up craving a drink. They don't need alcohol to function. They might even take breaks, do 'Dry January', or set rules like 'only on weekends'. But deep down, they feel a subtle tension. A sense that alcohol is taking more than it's giving. They might tell themselves they should be able to moderate, but that moderation feels exhausting. They cycle through rules, bargains and negotiations, trying to keep alcohol in its place – only to find that it soon creeps back in.

You might relate to grey area drinking if:

- You don't drink every day, but when you do, it's more than you intended.
- You toggle between productive days and hungover, unproductive days.
- You can stop drinking for relatively short periods (a few weeks, even a few months), but staying stopped is the hard part.
- Alcohol doesn't feel like an issue, yet you know you're more dependent on it than you'd like – and this is subtly affecting your energy, relationships, or self-trust.
- You have one small, internal voice telling you to stop drinking, but another that's telling you to stop overthinking it… it'll be fine.

Recognising this space isn't about labels. It's about self-awareness, no matter where you are on the spectrum.

The real challenge of grey area drinking isn't just the drinking itself – it's the denial and confusion that come with it. Because you don't fit the stereotype of an addict, you tell yourself everything is fine. Because you can go without it, you convince yourself it's not a problem. And yet… there's that whisper of something being off. A feeling that alcohol is dulling your edges, keeping you stuck in patterns that don't quite align with the person you want to be.

BREAKING THE BINARY

Not only is binary thinking outdated, it is harmfully reductive. It oversimplifies a complex relationship into a moral diagnosis. It ignores the vast and growing number of people – the grey area drinkers – who may not fit the stereotype.

What Jolene Parks does so powerfully is bring nuance back into the conversation. She names the emotional drivers behind so much grey area drinking – the stress, the anxiety, the dysregulated nervous systems we're trying to soothe. Her work doesn't pathologise drinking; it contextualises it.

Instead of asking 'What's wrong with you?', it asks a different question: 'What's your body trying to manage?' It highlights the role of alcohol as a self-soothing tool for people who are often high-functioning but inwardly depleted – running on adrenaline, craving connection and rarely feeling safe enough to slow down.

It's not about weakness. It's about unmet needs – and learning to address these in healthier, more sustainable ways.

Jolene's work gives people permission to explore their relationship with alcohol before it becomes a crisis. It invites reflection without shame, offering a language that feels compassionate instead of clinical. And in doing so, it highlights something essential:

- That you don't have to hit rock bottom to have a problem.
- You don't have to wait for things to get 'bad enough' to want better.

So, let's stop with unhelpful labels (like 'alcoholic') which turn a behaviour into an identity, draw a line between 'us' and 'them', and create shame, stigma and silence. Yes, we might use words like 'shopaholic' to describe people who can't stop shopping, or 'workaholic' for those who compulsively work excessively long hours, but here's the difference: we don't attach this label and then decide that's who they are for life. We recognise that people can fall into unhealthy patterns – and also change.

Letting go of labels

So if not labels… then what?

What the medical world now offers is something far more useful – and far more humane. Instead of dividing people into 'normal drinkers' and 'problem drinkers', the Alcohol Use Disorder (AUD) framework recognises that drinking exists on a spectrum. It doesn't ask, 'Are you an alcoholic?' but rather, 'How is alcohol impacting your life – right now?'

The criteria are simple, clear and behaviour-based – not identity-based. They're designed to reflect the wide range of ways alcohol can affect us, from mild disruption to severe dependence. And they remind us that it's not about a single moment of failure. It's about patterns. And patterns can be changed.

The behaviour-based criteria for AUD include:

- **Loss of control** – Drinking more or for longer than intended.

- **Failed attempts to cut back** – Wanting to drink less but struggling to do so.
- **Time consumption** – Spending excessive time drinking or recovering.
- **Cravings** – Feeling strong urges to drink.
- **Role impairment** – Alcohol affecting responsibilities at work, home or school.
- **Social impact** – Drinking despite it damaging relationships.
- **Abandoning activities** – Losing interest in hobbies or passions.
- **Risky situations** – Drinking in physically dangerous situations (e.g. driving).
- **Health risks** – Continuing to drink despite negative health effects.
- **Tolerance** – Needing more alcohol to feel the same effects.
- **Withdrawal** – Experiencing physical or emotional symptoms without alcohol.

If you meet two or more of these criteria within a 12-month period, you likely have AUD.

- Mild: 2–3 criteria
- Moderate: 4–5 criteria
- Severe: 6 or more criteria

Put simply: the more criteria you meet, the deeper alcohol's hold on you. FYI, I was a solid 'severe'. But what's important is that nowhere on this scale does a buzzer go off to declare that you've crossed the line into 'alcoholic' territory. There's no border crossing, no moment where you leave the land of normal drinkers and enter some irreversible 'alcoholic' fate.

If you're on the spectrum, you're not broken. Because here's the thing: alcohol is an addictive substance. No one is immune. And the only label you need identify with is being human.

From labels to liberation

Understanding the Alcohol Use Disorder spectrum isn't just about identifying behaviours – it's about reclaiming agency.

Most people don't fit neatly into boxes, but we can all ask the incredibly useful and compassionate question: 'Is alcohol helping me thrive, or is it standing in my way?'

Recognising grey area drinking is powerful because it shifts the conversation from rock bottom to potential. You stop measuring your drinking against whether it's creating chaos and disaster, and start measuring it against whether it is creating a barrier to your dreams, your health, your happiness. And that's where real transformation begins. Not from a place of punishment or loss, but from a place of possibility.

Because even if your drinking isn't chaotic or disruptive – it could still be quietly holding you back.

And that's something worth thinking about.

UNDERSTANDING THE NATURE OF YOUR DRINKING

While alcohol use exists on a spectrum, understanding *why* you drink is one of the most powerful insights you can gain.

For some, drinking is predominantly habitual i.e. a learned behaviour that's been repeated so many times, it's almost automatic. A routine, like scrolling on your phone when you're bored, or automatically flicking the kettle on in the morning. It's not driven by a strong craving, but by familiarity. It happens without much thought, often in specific settings or at certain times. Habits like this tend to be situational – but that doesn't mean they're meaningless. They often serve a quiet purpose: easing boredom, creating structure, marking a transition in the day, or gently soothing low-level stress. The emotional need might not shout loudly – but it's still there, quietly shaping behaviour.

For others, alcohol has taken on a bigger role. It's no longer just part of the background routine – it's the CEO. The one calling the shots.

In this case, drinking isn't just a habit. It's become a coping mechanism – a way to self-soothe, escape or manage difficult emotions. Whether it's stress, sadness, anger or emptiness, alcohol steps in to smooth the edges or numb the discomfort.

And it's when drinking is providing relief, comfort, or emotional regulation, that you start to move into the territory of dependence. You might not always feel desperate for it – but you notice its absence. You rely on it, consciously or not, to get through. To cope. To feel OK.

Again, this is not about labels, and it's also not about *how much* you drink. It's about the role alcohol plays in your life. The same amount of alcohol can be a harmless routine for one person, but a dependency trigger for another.

The difference often lies in what happens when it's taken away:

- If your drinking is mostly habitual, you might notice its absence in terms of the missing ritual or routine – but life will continue without major disruption. Stopping drinking might feel a little strange at first, be a bit discomforting, as in: where's that thing I'm used to having? You might need to make a shift in schedule, or even a conscious decision to replace the drink with something else. But it won't leave a deep emotional imprint.

- If alcohol is providing emotional relief, removing it can feel deeply unsettling. Like losing a crutch or knocking away a piece of scaffolding. The discomfort goes beyond inconvenience – it can show up as restlessness, anxiety, mood swings or strong cravings. You may even notice physical symptoms. Not because you lack willpower, but because alcohol has been doing a job – and now that job isn't being done. In this case, there will be work to do that is partly about drinking less, and partly about learning new ways to cope, self-soothe, and regulate emotions.

Interestingly, while the line between habit and dependence can blur, clinicians and neuroscientists agree that not all habits involve addiction – but all dependencies involve some loss of control.

This distinction between habit and dependency isn't just theoretical. It has real-world implications for how we approach change. While the surface behaviour may look the same (pouring a drink at the end of the day, reaching for a glass in social settings), the underlying mechanisms can be very different. Here's a simple breakdown of the key differences:

Habit	Dependency
Largely under conscious control	Often uncontrollable (compulsions)
No physical or psychological reliance	Can involve physical and psychological reliance
Impact may be neutral or positive	Impact is usually harmful

Habit	Dependency
Minimal brain changes occur	Significant changes in brain chemistry occur (e.g. reward pathways)

If your drinking is mostly habitual, the good news is that you're likely not reliant on alcohol to feel okay. You've just formed a pattern. And patterns can be changed.

If your drinking leans towards dependency, this doesn't mean you're 'a lost cause', but it does mean alcohol has a deeper hold on you than mere routine. Your brain has started at a deep level to link drinking with relief, which inevitably involves some loss of control.

No 'right' or 'wrong'

There is no 'good' or 'bad', 'right' or 'wrong' here. The idea is simply to try to recognise what's at play, so you can approach change with the right tools.

In the third section of this book, we will go a bit deeper into habit change – how to tweak behaviours, shift routines, and make drinking a conscious choice rather than an automatic one. For those of you who feel your drinking is filling emotional gaps, the same section will introduce tools for emotional growth and self-reflection, which can help address what job alcohol is doing for you in the first place.

As I say, one isn't better than the other. They're just different paths to the same destination: a more conscious, intentional relationship with alcohol, where you're in control, not the other way around.

In the next chapter, we'll take a closer look at what's really driving your choice to drink – and what it means to take back the wheel.

KEY TAKE-AWAYS:

- Drinking isn't binary. It exists on a spectrum, and many people sit within a grey area where drinking isn't dramatic – but it often creates quiet confusion, subtle self-doubt, and a sense that alcohol is taking more than it's giving.
- The fear of labels keeps people stuck – letting go of the term 'alcoholic' allows for self-reflection without judgement.
- The medical world now recognises the sliding scale of Alcohol Use Disorder (AUD), replacing outdated, black-and-white thinking.
- Understanding whether your drinking is habit-driven or emotionally driven is key to knowing what kind of change will be most effective.
- There's no right or wrong path. Only different approaches to creating a life where alcohol no longer holds you back.

Food for thought:

1. **What would you actually miss if alcohol disappeared from your life?**

   Is it the ritual, the relief – or the buffer it gives you from harder feelings?

2. **Do you have an internal dialogue with yourself about alcohol?**

   Are you constantly negotiating with yourself – setting limits, making rules or justifying your drinking?

3. **If alcohol wasn't an option, how would you handle stress, celebration or boredom?**

   Do you have other tools in place, or does alcohol feel like your default coping mechanism?

4. **If you reframed alcohol as medicine – something that alters your mind and body – would you still drink it as freely?**

   Would you so readily reach for a glass of wine if you saw it as taking a dose of a drug?

5. **What would your life look like if you had full agency over your drinking?**

   How would it feel to be in complete control, rather than having alcohol calling the shots?

Relevant podcast episodes:

Episode 3. Why Less is More

Episode 31. From Grey Area Drinking to Holistic Health

Episode 54. Breaking the Alcohol Cycle – Habits vs Dependency

CHAPTER 6

THE GREAT DISCONNECT

Before we go any further, let's return briefly to the idea of alcohol as the Chief Emotions Officer. It's a role many of us have quietly handed over to drink – sometimes for years – asking it to manage our stress, silence our doubts, amplify our joy or soften our pain. But while alcohol might temporarily numb what we feel, it also gradually disconnects us from ourselves. Because this CEO doesn't just manage emotions in a quick-fix, half-arsed way. It takes our feelings before they even reach us, intercepts them and meddles with their messages. Unfortunately, when we drink too much, we're not just outsourcing a simple task. We are outsourcing our very ability to feel, process and grow.

In dulling discomfort, we are also dulling everything else. Our clarity, our intuition, our own awareness – the one thing that could truly guide us.

THE PYRAMID OF AWARENESS

To understand how alcohol disconnects us, we need to understand the way our mind processes emotions.

Emotions don't just 'happen', they have layers. We experience something, we react, and beneath that reaction lies a deeper response. When we drink, however, we are kept stuck at the surface level, alcohol preventing us from ever getting to the truth underneath.

When he came on to the podcast, Dr Manoj Krishna (public speaker and founder of HappierMe) explained how we can grow by processing negative emotions.

Stage 1 – External events/trigger: something happens in the outside world (e.g. we receive criticism, experience rejection, or feel overwhelmed.)

Stage 2 – Immediate thoughts and reactions: we feel discomfort (e.g. frustration, sadness, stress, anger).

Stage 3 – Self-awareness: if we pause instead of reacting, we can observe our thoughts, process our emotions, understand our reactions and shift our responses. This is where real growth happens.

The problem is that when alcohol is part of our emotional management system, we never reach the vital third stage of self-awareness. Instead of observing our thoughts and understanding our reactions, we numb our emotions. So, alcohol keeps us stuck at stage 2, where growth remains elusive. We feel anxious, we drink. We feel lonely, we drink. We never go deeper to ask what's behind this feeling? Where did it start? We just keep pressing mute. And when we mute emotions for long enough, we don't just silence the bad ones – we lose connection with the whole shebang: joy, excitement, self-trust, purpose. It all gets diluted in the same way. So we end up simply feeling less.

THE DISCONNECTION DILEMMA

I have come to think of emotions as an internal postal service, delivering vital messages about our needs, boundaries and desires. That sharp pang of sadness is trying to tell us something. That feeling of overwhelm is carrying a message that we've over-committed. The feeling of guilt is conveying that we've done something misaligned to our values. That simmering frustration holds another valuable insight. But when we let alcohol step in as our middleman, those messages get lost in transit.

Without access to our emotions, we become disconnected from ourselves. We don't just numb the painful feelings, we also blunt the joyful ones. We live in a dulled-down version of our own lives, like watching a film with the brightness turned down. And what's worse, we forget that it was ever supposed to be any different.

Emotions are the essence of what makes us human. They are the colour in our experiences, the music behind our stories, the force that drives us to love, to create, to care and to connect. When we suppress them, we risk living on autopilot. Simply drifting through life without ever truly engaging with it.

Over time, this emotional dulling can lead to a creeping sense of emptiness. We might not even recognise it at first; we just know that things feel… flat. Exciting moments don't sparkle the way they used to. We stop noticing the beauty in little things. Relationships can feel a little lacking and uninteresting.

And then, having done our best to turn the volume down on all our painful emotions, we stop listening altogether. And when we stop listening, we stop knowing what we truly need and value.

Silencing the uncomfortable feeling of loneliness, for example, means we miss want we want (e.g. physical touch and connection), what we need (e.g. to be around people) and what, at our core, we cherish – close relationships.

Being so adrift means we may stay in jobs that drain us, relationships that don't fulfil us, and routines that don't serve us – all because the signals that would have guided us to change are being silenced. Without our emotions lighting the way, we become lost travellers without a compass, stuck in a life that doesn't quite feel like our own.

Laura Bartlett, entrepreneur and inspirational speaker, summed it up when she came on to the podcast, saying: 'Alcohol suppresses your spirit – the little whisper that you have from your soul, which is always so quiet because it's trying to shout amongst the loud noise of the negativity.'

EMOTIONAL LITERACY

It's fair to say that if emotions were a language, very few of us might be described as fluent. Historically, British culture in particular has prized restraint, stoicism and self-control. Emotional expression – especially anything perceived as dramatic, needy or vulnerable – has tended to be viewed as a weakness or an embarrassment. It's an ethos that has roots in Victorian ideals of propriety and self-discipline, post-war attitudes of 'stiff upper lip' survivalism, boarding school culture (where independence and emotional suppression were seen as maturity) and class-based dynamics, where maintaining a certain social image meant hiding inner struggles.

Alcohol, ever the eager CEO, encourages us to bunk off our emotional language class altogether. Instead of learning how to sit with discomfort and find ways to articulate it, we reach for a drink. Instead of processing stress, we press the 'mute' button. Instead of developing resilience, we outsource the hard work.

But, as we have seen, emotional literacy isn't just about handling pain. It's also about feeling excitement, understanding love, deepening self-awareness. When we hand over the reins to alcohol, we don't just avoid the tough stuff; we rob ourselves of the full spectrum of human experience.

The emotion wheel, developed by psychologists to help us identify and process our feelings, categorises emotions into primary feelings such as joy, sadness, fear, anger, surprise and disgust – each of which branches into dozens of more nuanced emotions, from serenity to grief, and excitement to shame. In total, there are hundreds of emotions, both positive and negative, that shape us and the way we live.

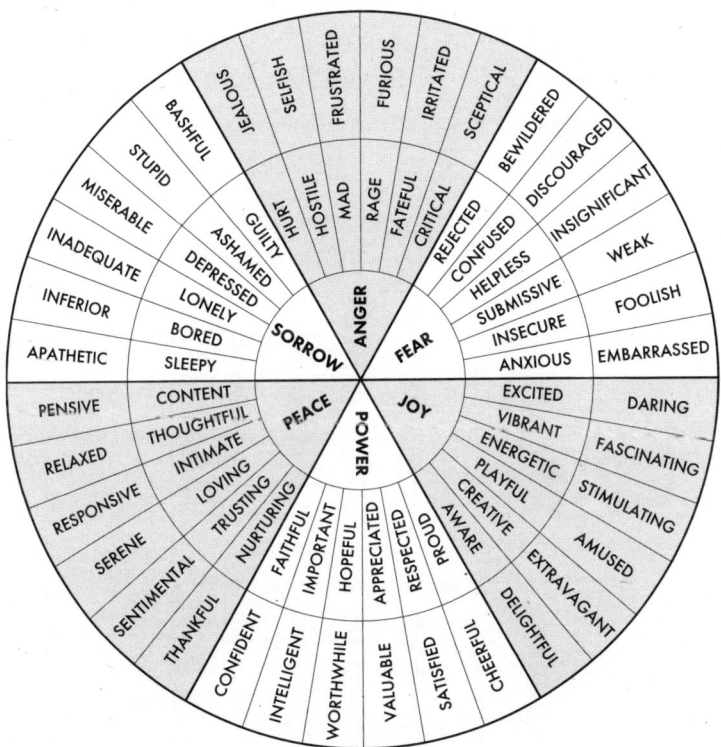

The wheel, as you can see, is detailed. However, alcohol doesn't really do details. It's not a precision tool.

When we drink to ease stress, to dull sadness, or to take the edge off anger, we don't get to brief the CEO by saying:

- Could you please take away my anxiety, but leave my confidence intact.

- Maybe numb my loneliness, but let me still feel deep joy.
- Quieten my sadness, but keep my excitement alive.

Alcohol flattens the whole emotional landscape. And over time, this flattening effect disconnects us from ourselves, leaving us in a place where nothing feels truly bad… but nothing feels truly great either.

Alcohol can't target specific emotions:

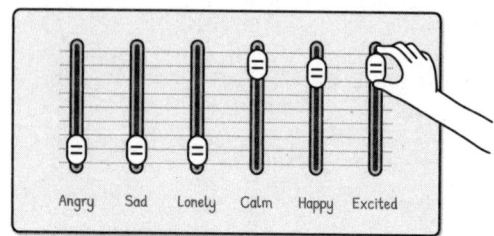

Instead, it numbs them all:

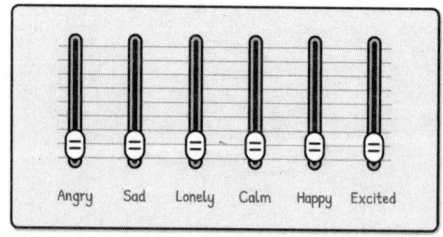

If we want to reclaim real happiness, real connection and real resilience, we have to learn how to feel *everything*, not just the easy stuff. We've got to feel the difficult things too. Because emotions aren't the enemy. They are messages, guiding us towards what matters most.

When we remain emotionally illiterate, we struggle to name our feelings, let alone understand them. Instead of recognising that we're feeling lonely, we might just feel 'off'. Instead of realising we're overwhelmed and need rest, we push forward. Without the ability to identify our emotions, we lose the ability to respond to them in ways that could actually help us.

There is no relationship more important than the one you have with yourself. In an episode of the podcast, when I spoke to Christy Osborne, sobriety coach and author of *Love Life Sober*, she observed that whatever spirituality means to people, it involves connecting to something, often yourself, on a deep level… and this is very hard to do when you're drinking.

Emotional disconnection also affects our relationships, big time. When we don't have the words for our feelings, communication breaks down. We may lash out instead of expressing frustration, withdraw instead of seeking comfort, or avoid conversations that could lead to growth. Many people think of alcohol as something that brings them closer to others, but in reality it actually makes us more self-focused, more withdrawn and less present.

Over time, emotional illiteracy means we miss out on something fundamental: the ability to evolve. Emotions are meant to guide us, shape us and teach us. If we never learn to read them, we stagnate, staying stuck in patterns that don't serve us, making the same mistakes, feeling the same frustrations, and never quite understanding why.

HOW TO BE A MAN

From an early age, we're subtly (and sometimes explicitly) taught which emotions are acceptable and which are not. And for men, the message can be particularly clear and damaging, as Alex Clapp (founder of Claritee, an organisation that delivers exceptional and entertaining sober corporate events) highlights: 'I can't remember ever being asked how I felt as a child. A man had to be strong, not show emotion, and cope with anything thrown at him. I've still never seen my dad cry.'

It's a societal thing again – a historical culture of bravado that has created a certain male stereotype. Traditionally, phrases like 'man up', 'grow a pair' and 'don't be such a girl' have reinforced the idea that sensitivity is unmanly.

'I plodded along through life with this belief that men don't cry,' said Alex, 'and when I started experiencing serious health issues, I just pretended everything was fine. I'd joke about it. If you make people laugh, they don't ask deeper questions.'

Alcohol can be an excellent accomplice in the general mission of cover-up. By numbing our emotions, it effectively enables us to hide from the world – to keep functioning on the surface, maintaining the illusion that everything is fine, while denying the true feelings within. This was the case for Alex: 'To the outside world, I was functioning fine. But inside, I was a little lost boy who had never processed his emotions.'

And, as he discovered, with this illusion of functionality,

the disconnection just grew. Slowly, for him, alcohol moved from being an occasional relief to an everyday necessity.

'It went from drinking a few nights a week, to every night, to heavier drinking, to drinking in the afternoons, to waking up needing vodka first thing in the morning. My brain was telling me this wasn't a problem. That this was survival.'

Alcohol all too easily becomes the silent confessional; a way to self-medicate against painful emotions, without ever having to acknowledge them. But when emotions have no outlet, they don't disappear. They get buried, and then often end up resurfacing in unhealthy ways.

Thankfully, younger generations are becoming increasingly emotionally literate. Therapy is normalised today, conversations about mental health are encouraged and showing vulnerability is seen as a sign of strength rather than weakness. The young are rejecting the just-get-on-with-it mentality and instead advocating for authenticity, openness and connection. And that's a significant shift, because emotional literacy isn't just about naming feelings; it's about breaking generational cycles of silence.

Alex, now in recovery, is helping to shift this cultural conditioning. 'I teach boxing these days, and one of the most important things we do is ask kids how they're feeling. We check in. We talk.'

This is how the cycle changes. The more we normalise emotional expression, especially for boys and young men, the less they'll need to rely on alcohol as an emotional crutch later in life. 'I see my son and his friends tell each other how they feel,' concluded Alex, 'and it gives me hope.'

THE FULFILMENT ILLUSION

In my twenties and thirties, I certainly wasn't a spiritual person. I wasn't searching for deeper meaning or trying to understand myself on any profound level. I was living for the laughs and the giggles, absorbed in a world of fun, self-indulgence, and social validation. And I don't apologise for that, because for many people, that's exactly what that stage of life looks like.

At that time, I didn't feel connected to anything bigger than myself. My world revolved around what felt good in the moment – the next big night out, the latest new, trendy bar in Soho, the next slightly gung-ho adventure. I was the main character in my life, and my only real goal was to keep the good times rolling.

That said, exciting as it all seemed, that bravado moment was fleeting. The things I was chasing (status, social life, the buzz of belonging) felt like they should make me happy. And yet, there I was, often hungover, restless and empty. Looking back, I see that even at that stage alcohol was doing a lot of heavy lifting for me, fuelling the social whirlwind, masking deeper discontent, filling the space where self-reflection might have lived.

By reinforcing self-absorption, alcohol can inflate our ego. It keeps us focused on ourselves, our wants, our social currency. And when we drink, we're often not fully present for others. We become wrapped up in our own emotions, reactions and experiences, mistaking that self-focus for fulfilment. True connection, whether with other people, with a purpose or something bigger than ourselves, requires stepping outside of our own bubble, while alcohol keeps us firmly trapped inside it.

This is why having children hit me like a ton of bricks. I was in my mid-thirties, living that life I have just described, and suddenly life wasn't all about me any more.

For the first time, I was connected to something truly bigger than myself. It was one almighty wake-up call. A shift from ego to responsibility, from self-indulgence to something infinitely more meaningful. And in that shift, I started to see just how hollow my previous pursuits had been.

Except I wasn't quite ready for it.

Motherhood demands humility, selflessness and patience – all qualities that I hadn't exactly been building in my drinking years. Instead, I had been falling in and out of bars for a decade, fine-tuning my ability to handle emotions with alcohol, failing to actually process them. And now, with a baby in my arms, I felt ill-equipped for this role that required everything I had never practised.

I wish I could say I adapted easily, but as you know by now, I really struggled with my first few years of motherhood. I wasn't ready to put someone else first. I resented the loss of freedom, the exhaustion, the relentless responsibility. And when evening came, alcohol was right there, ready to help me escape, to provide me with the (false) sense of fulfilment I thought I needed to compensate for the emptiness I had felt all day.

THE WISDOM WE IGNORE

Intuition is a quiet but powerful voice within us, guiding us towards what is right and away from what is wrong. It warns us when something feels off, and helps us course-correct when needed.

Think of intuition as your inner mentor: the wise, compassionate guide who knows you better than anyone else – who tells you when you're heading in the wrong direction, when you're ignoring your deepest needs, and when you're settling for less than you deserve.

The thing is, though, that intuition requires space and silence to be heard. And when alcohol is the CEO, intuition is the employee that never gets a word in. When we constantly reach for a drink to drown out discomfort, we also drown out our inner voice. And over time, it becomes quieter, until one day, we no longer hear it at all.

The reason why this is a problem is that when we silence our intuition, we also lose our ability to trust ourselves. Without it, we become rudderless, making decisions based on external pressures rather than internal wisdom.

We second-guess choices, struggle to make out minds up about things and become more susceptible to outside influence. Instead of confidently navigating life, we stumble through it, unsure of who we are or what we truly want. This can lead to a life that feels misaligned, where we wake up years later wondering how the hell we got so far away from what we once dreamed of.

But perhaps the greatest tragedy of all is that we stop

believing that the wisdom was ever there in the first place. We forget that we ever had access to this deep, inner knowing. And without that belief, we don't even attempt to reconnect with it.

Nothing highlighted this more to me than when my first daughter was born. About a month after we brought her home from the hospital, I vividly remember my mum coming to stay for a week. One day my baby girl was crying in her Moses basket and I just stood there, looking through a parenting book, desperately trying to work out what might be wrong. I was crying, too, frantically flicking through this book, completely lost and looking for clues. And I remember my mum saying to me, 'Anna, what are you doing? Put the damn book down. You're not going to find the answers in a book.'

Through my sobbing I told her that I didn't know what I needed to do, and as she gently prised the book out of my hand, she simply said, 'You do. You know how to do this, but you're not listening. You're not listening to your own intuition. You've got a mother's instinct, but you're not listening to it.'

I remember thinking, 'I don't. I don't have that.' I couldn't hear anything. I couldn't hear the answers coming. I didn't believe they were there.

I know with all my heart, looking back now, that I was literally disconnected. Disconnected from that inner compass that we have, disconnected from any wisdom, any sort of internal mentorship, or instinct. It had just gone. And I was looking for how to raise my baby in the pages of a book.

My mum was basically asking me to trust myself and to know that I had the answers. That they would come to me if I let them and that I would grow into this role, even if I hadn't slipped naturally into it the moment I brought my daughter home.

STUNTED EMOTIONAL GROWTH

I am a firm believer that it is almost impossible to grow emotionally when you're drinking to manage your feelings. If you're trying *not* to feel the very things you need to feel, you're just not going to find those breakthroughs.

Alcohol stunts you. When I reached for that book as I stood over my crying baby, it was for yet another quick fix, a way of avoiding – or at least delaying – the work that needed to be done.

Alex's recovery journey revealed just how much emotional work he had avoided: 'I spent two days in bed after one therapy session, because my body was so drained from finally letting emotions out.'

Growth happens in the moments when we sit with our feelings, however uncomfortable they may be. The breakup grief, the work stress, the existential dread. These are the storms that make us resilient, wise and deeply human. Imagine a tree that never faces wind or a storm. It might grow, but it won't be strong. It won't develop the deep roots it needs to withstand challenges. That's what happens when alcohol shields us from emotional discomfort.

When we dodge our emotions, we don't grow. And without growth, we remain stuck in outdated emotional patterns, responding to life with the same limited tools we've always used. We never develop the ability to self-soothe, to adapt or truly heal. And as a result, we risk never reaching emotional fluency at all.

TAKING THE BLINDFOLD OFF

Discovery is an active process. It requires curiosity (there's that word again), exploration and a willingness to engage with the unknown. Emotional discovery (understanding who we are and what truly matters to us) is no different.

But when alcohol stands in the way, it's like trying to explore a landscape with a blindfold on. It prevents us from asking important questions, like: Why do I react this way? What do I truly want? What is this discomfort trying to teach me? Instead of leaning into these questions, we drink over them. We avoid the difficult, yet necessary, inner work that leads to genuine resilience and self-understanding.

Resilience is about learning how to cope with adversity – it's forged in the moments we face hardship head-on, confronting pain, learning from it, and realising our emotions can't hurt us.

Without it, and an understanding of our own strength, we are easily afraid. Small setbacks feel catastrophic, and challenges seem insurmountable. We lose confidence in our ability to handle life's difficulties because we've never allowed ourselves to prove that we can. And over time, this fragile emotional state can lead to increased anxiety, fear of discomfort and a chronic sense of vulnerability.

And the cost is a life lived on the surface. When we avoid emotional discovery, we miss out on the deeper layers of our identity. We remain strangers to our own inner world, disconnected from our purpose and potential. True emotional discovery requires bravery. The courage to sit with uncomfortable feelings, and to embrace the messy, beautiful process of growth.

PROBLEM... WHAT PROBLEM?

What if, instead of hiring alcohol as our Chief Emotions Officer, we reclaimed that role for ourselves? What if, instead of thinking of feelings as something to be feared or managed, we embraced them as the very things that lead us towards the lives we're meant to live?

For so long, we've been conditioned to believe that difficult emotions are problems to solve, glitches in an otherwise smooth existence. But what if they are, in fact, essential? What if sadness is a call to slow down and process, anger a signal that our boundaries are being crossed, fear an invitation to step forward with courage? What if our emotions, every single one of them, exist for a reason?

The good news is that we can relearn how to sit with our emotions, decode their messages, and reconnect with a full, unedited version of life. It's not always comfortable (true growth rarely is), but the rewards are profound.

When we stop outsourcing our feelings to alcohol, we take back our agency. We become fluent in the language of our own inner world. We move through life with a new sense of clarity, no longer numbed, no longer drifting.

And something remarkable happens when we do this: we start trusting ourselves again. We make decisions not from a place of avoidance but from alignment. We strengthen our resilience, knowing we can handle whatever life throws our way, without feeling like we have to escape it. We rediscover joy in its purest form, no longer muted or manufactured, but real, rich and deeply felt.

For years, I thought alcohol was the answer to everything. But when I stopped drinking, I was confronted with a bigger question: If alcohol isn't my go-to any more, then what is?

Christy described this perfectly: 'When you break free from alcohol, it's like, okay, well, what's my purpose? And why am I here? And what do I do with all this newfound time, energy and mental clarity? What do I feel drawn to do with it?'

When we stop running from our emotions, we start running towards our true selves. And that changes everything.

Sam Williams, an ADHD and menopause coach who I spoke to on the podcast, calls this process 'MEsearch' – the act of becoming deeply, relentlessly curious about ourselves. When she stopped drinking, she didn't just give up alcohol; she embarked on an exploration of who she really was without it.

Like so many of us, Sam had found herself drinking simply to try to manage life – juggling work, family and the everyday pressures. Alcohol was never something she questioned. It was just there. A way to unwind, a familiar habit. What she didn't realise was that it was also dulling her relationship with herself, to the extent of masking her ADHD. When Sam decided to take a break from drinking, she wasn't expecting a profound transformation. She was just curious. What would life feel like without alcohol? Could she really handle stress, emotions and social situations without it?

The answer surprised her.

The moment she removed alcohol, she realised how much of herself she had been missing. She suddenly had access to her own thoughts – unfiltered, uninterrupted and honest.

'A lot of people drink to lower their inhibitions, but I never really had that problem. For me, it was about quieting the thoughts in my head and giving myself some headspace. Drinking was the only time I could actually switch my brain off.'

For the first time in years, Sam could hear herself. At first, it was uncomfortable. Without wine to take the edge off, the emotions she had once numbed began surfacing. But instead of drowning them out, she chose to sit with them. To get curious about them. And in doing so, she reconnected with a version of herself that had long been buried under busy schedules and coping mechanisms.

And something else happened – self-awareness grew into self-love, and self-love grew into an abundance of love for others in her life.

'I didn't think it was possible to love my children any more than I already did. But I can tell you, I do. In loving myself, my heart has expanded to the point where I can love others more, with a depth and a trueness I hadn't managed before.'

That's the irony of alcohol. We often use it to connect more – to bond, to relax, to escape – but in reality, it cuts us off from the deepest connections of all.

Sam's story isn't about losing alcohol. It's about finding herself.

Curiosity reconnects us. The moment we stop regarding our emotions as problems to be solved and instead start recognising them as messages to be heard, everything changes.

KEY TAKE-AWAYS:

- We've been sold the idea that happiness is the goal. But in chasing constant happiness, we lose the ability to sit with discomfort and learn from it.
- Numbing emotions doesn't just silence pain – it mutes joy, clarity and purpose too. We don't get to choose what alcohol dulls; it blunts everything.
- Emotional suppression is cultural. Many of us – especially men – were taught to hide feelings, making alcohol a go-to coping tool.
- Alcohol silences intuition. It drowns out our inner wisdom and erodes self-trust, leaving us disconnected from what we truly need.

- Emotional literacy is a skill, not an innate trait. When we build it, we learn to recognise and name our feelings – rather than react to them or numb them.
- Alcohol stunts emotional growth, delaying resilience, self-awareness and connection. Curiosity changes everything. When we stop judging emotions and start observing them, they become signposts to deeper fulfilment.

Food for thought:

1. **When was the last time you sat with a difficult emotion rather than trying to escape or numb it?**
   What did it reveal to you?

2. **Have you ever mistaken alcohol for connection?**
   Think about times when you drank to feel closer to others – did it truly deepen your relationships?

3. **How has the cultural messaging around emotions and drinking influenced your own beliefs?**
   Have you internalised ideas like 'real men don't cry' or 'women should hold it together' – and how have those shaped your behaviours?

4. **If alcohol has been your 'go-to' for managing emotions, what alternative coping strategies could you explore?**
   How might it feel to approach discomfort with curiosity rather than avoidance?

5. **What would it mean for you to truly trust yourself?** How might your life change if you listened to your intuition instead of silencing it?

Relevant podcast episodes:
Episode 6. Raising the Bar Without Alcohol
Episode 19. Alcohol-Free Peace: Self-love, ADHD & Perimenopause
Episode 22. Overcoming Addiction and Redefining Masculinity
Episode 25. The Hidden Drivers of Behaviour and Addiction
Episode 44. Alcohol & Spiritual Growth
Episode 85. Waking Up to What Matters
Episode 86. From Alcohol to Radical Integrity
Episode 88. Family, Alcohol & The Power of Empathy

CHAPTER 7

THE HAPPINESS MYTH

Happiness and alcohol go hand in hand. At least, that's what we've been conditioned to believe.

From an early age, we're shown that drinking is the gateway to joy – the sparkling champagne at a wedding, the beer shared in celebration after a long day. Hollywood backs this up with glossy montages of friends laughing over drinks, bottles popped in moments of triumph, a weary protagonist sighing in relief as they take the first sip. The undiluted message is that drinking equals happiness.

And certainly, as a coach, when I start working with people and I ask them to talk to me about 'why' they drink, one of the most common answers is: 'Because it makes me happy.'

At face value, it makes sense. Alcohol gives us a buzz, a rush, a momentary lightness. The first drink can feel like a warm glow spreading through the body, a gentle lifting of the weight of the day. But as we now know, that feeling doesn't last. And moreover, once it fades, it doesn't leave us neutral, it leaves us lower than we were when we started.

If alcohol were truly making us happy, then drinking more would surely make us happier. And the people who drink the most – all day every day – should be living their best life.

But the reality is that we chase that initial fleeting high, only to find that it was never real in the first place – it was an artificial dump of dopamine that cannot be recaptured by subsequent drinks. In fact, the moment we reach for alcohol to create happiness, we're unknowingly reaching for a wrecking-ball to demolish the very foundation of our well-being.

If happiness is a lightbulb, then alcohol is the dimmer switch – turning down our lows, yes, but also dulling every bright, beautiful, authentic moment in the process.

So if alcohol isn't the source of happiness, what is?

And why have we spent so long believing otherwise?

'I'LL BE HAPPY WHEN...'

If there's one thing we humans are exceptionally good at, it's postponing happiness.

From childhood, we're handed an invisible checklist of achievements that are supposed to unlock it. Work hard, get good exam grades, land a stable job, buy a house, find a partner, have kids, build wealth... then, finally, you'll be happy. We learn to treat joy as something always on the horizon, always one step away, always contingent on us reaching the next milestone and ticking the next box.

This isn't just an individual mindset. It's a cultural epidemic. We live in a world that constantly dangles happiness in front of us like a carrot on a stick, leading us forwards but never allowing us to grasp it. Consumerism, a self-improvement culture, social media... all thrive on the idea that we're not quite there yet.

- You'll be happy when you get the promotion.
- You'll be happy when you lose the weight.
- You'll be happy when you meet 'the one'.
- You'll be happy when you have more money, more success, more recognition.

And when we do achieve those things? The goalposts seem to move.

It's what psychologists call the Hedonic Treadmill – the endless cycle of chasing external rewards, only to find that the happiness they bring is fleeting, forcing us to run after the next one. We're conditioned to believe that our contentment is something to be earned, rather than something that can be experienced right now. For some, this frustration leads to restless striving – pushing harder, achieving more, hoping that somewhere along the way, fulfilment will finally click into place. I think that was me.

For others, it leads to numbing. Because when happiness feels out of reach, the quickest fix is to bypass the chase altogether, and to manufacture the feeling instead. Alcohol, social media, shopping, food, gambling, workaholism... All offer temporary relief from the gnawing sense that something is missing. So the restless striving and the numbing can go hand in hand.

But here's the thing: happiness isn't waiting at some future destination. It isn't hidden in the next big purchase, the next life upgrade, the next external validation.

Why? Because we're not actually seeking happiness. We're seeking escape from the discomfort of its absence.

And when we don't feel as happy as we think we should, we blame ourselves. We assume we're failing at life, rather than realising that the entire framework we were given was flawed to begin with.

So, if happiness isn't found in chasing, and it isn't found in numbing, where does it come from?

THE SCIENCE OF HAPPINESS

For centuries, philosophers and scientists have studied what truly makes us happy.

Abraham Maslow

In 1943, this renowned psychologist introduced his famous Hierarchy of Needs. His framework is beautifully simple, and has stood the test of time, despite the occasional, suggested revision. It's a pyramid, basically, illustrating the fundamental building blocks of human fulfilment.

- At the base, we have basic physiological, survival needs (food, water, safety).
- With these in place, we can aspire to move up to the next layer, which is about our need to feel physically safe.
- Again, attaining this sense of safety allows us to aspire

to the layer above, i.e. our social need for love, belonging and acceptance.
- Next, we move on to self-esteem. At this point, we don't just want to be part of the group, we want to be admired and celebrated within it.
- And then finally, at the top, at the pinnacle of the pyramid, sits self-actualisation, the highest form of human happiness, driven by purpose, creativity and deep connection.

SELF-ACTUALISATION
Finally, now our core needs are met, we're ready to pursue our deepest desire for self-actualisation – to become the most complete and authentic version of ourselves. With the fundamentals taken care of, we're free to act as we choose, aligned with our values and higher purpose.

SELF ESTEEM
Once we're secure in our social needs, our primal desires for status and self esteem come into play. We want to feel not only 'part of the group' – but an admired and respected part.

SOCIAL
If we feel safe, then our social needs for love and belonging come into play. We feel secure when we're part of a tribe we can trust and unworried about rejection or alienation.

SAFETY
If we feel OK in this exact moment, we then also want to feel safe: confident we can avoid pain, hunger and other dangers for the immediate future.

PHYSIOLOGICAL
At the very least, we don't want to be hungry, thirsty, exhausted, freezing, overheated, sick, or in pain.

So where does alcohol fit into this scheme of things? It doesn't. Alcohol systematically weakens every level of the pyramid.

MASLOW'S LEVEL	WHAT FUELS HAPPINESS?	HOW ALCOHOL UNDERMINES IT
Basic Needs (Sleep, Health, Safety)	Feeling well-rested, physically strong and secure.	Disrupts sleep, damages health, impairs judgement, increases risks.
Belonging & Connection (Love, Friendship, Community)	Deep relationships, emotional closeness, trust.	Creates false connection, leads to misunderstandings, emotional distance and regret.
Esteem & Self-Worth (Status, Respect, Admiration)	Confidence, mastery, a sense of accomplishment.	Causes self-doubt, lowers self-respect and fuels cycles of guilt and shame.
Self-Actualization (Purpose, Growth, Fulfilment)	Living in alignment with our values, pursuing meaningful goals.	Keeps people stuck in avoidance, delaying growth, numbing true desires.

This means that every time we reach for alcohol to 'enhance' happiness, we're actually chipping away at the very things that create it.

When I worked in advertising, my agency decided that it wanted to measure employee happiness and engagement. As Director of Strategy, I was tasked with implementing this survey, as having a happy and engaged staff was viewed to be key to success in pretty much every area of the business, from productivity to retention. I resolved that our approach should be grounded in neuroscience and emotional intelligence, i.e. that we would look beyond surface-level satisfaction metrics. So we used The Happiness Index, a survey co-founded by Matt Phelan, which is used by all sorts of companies and organisations to measure staff well-being, by asking them how they feel about their work and how this proliferates out into their wider daily lives.

What we discovered through the survey was eye-opening, if not entirely surprising. While many people said they were engaged in their work on the surface, their emotional data told a more complicated story. Feelings of stress, disconnection and not feeling truly heard or recognised were far more common than we'd expected. And clearly our team wasn't alone in this.

More recently, I invited Matt on to the podcast to talk about the science behind the data that his business has now gathered from millions of people across the world, and it corroborated what we found – that there is consistently this gap between what leaders think people are feeling, and what people actually feel day to day. It turns out that happiness at work isn't just about perks or productivity – it's about emotional safety, human connection, and the sense that what you do actually matters. Things that are hard to measure on a spreadsheet.

I loved Matt's corroboration of Maslow's theory that 'Nothing that makes us happy has been invented in the last 1,000 years'. Not money, not new technology, not flash cars. Love, connection, purpose, meaning, presence… these are the timeless, unchanging pillars of happiness – and, as we have seen, alcohol actively sabotages all of them. Ask yourself the following questions. When you drink too much:

- How many deep, meaningful conversations have been lost to arguments?
- How many personal goals have been delayed because of hangovers and regret?
- How many ambitions have been derailed by a lack of self-trust?
- How many moments of peace, clarity and gratitude have been hijacked by alcohol's numbing effect?

Alcohol doesn't bring us closer to real happiness, it distracts us from pursuing it.

Barbara Fredrickson

As we explore the science of happiness, we need to talk about Barbara, a professor at the University of North Carolina and one of the leading experts in the field of positive psychology. Her research looks at the concept of happiness in a scientific and objective way. Until the early 1990s, no one had really done this and her work is still thought by leading professionals to be the most comprehensive in its field.

Barbara posits that there are ten positive emotions, which combine to create the overall emotion that we call 'happiness'. Namely:

- **Joy** – the light, energising feeling that bubbles up when we're fully present in a moment of delight or pleasure.
- **Serenity** – the deep sense of inner peace, calm and safety, often felt when we're grounded and untroubled.
- **Gratitude** – the warm recognition of the good in our lives, and the appreciation for others or life itself.
- **Love** – that feeling of deep connection, trust and mutual care that bonds us to others in meaningful ways.
- **Hope** – the quiet belief that things can get better, even when we're facing difficulty or uncertainty.
- **Pride** – that satisfying sense of accomplishment that comes from effort, growth or doing something that aligns with our values.
- **Amusement** – the joy of humour, playfulness or shared laughter that lightens the mood and lifts the spirit.
- **Inspiration** – a spark that awakens us to new possibilities, ideas or ways of being – often through witnessing the best in others.
- **Awe** – a feeling of wonder and humility in the face of something vast, beautiful or beyond our understanding.
- **Interest** – the curiosity that draws us in, keeps us engaged and makes us want to explore or learn more.

Needless to say, alcohol doesn't amplify these emotions – instead it often dulls, distorts or delays them. For example, it can scramble serenity into anxiety, turn gratitude into regret. It can block the deep connection that love requires and cloud the future that hope depends on. It can turn pride into self-criticism and evaporate inspiration. The very states that make life feel rich and worth living can be eroded.

The good news? In this list of sustainable happiness 'drivers', there is nothing about buying new cars, or new wardrobes or material things. Just a list of emotional qualities that we all have the power to cultivate within ourselves. Which is bloody brilliant news, no? We cannot necessarily change our external environment, but we can absolutely influence what's going on for us inside. We all – each and every one of us – have the power to make changes internally that could make us happy. In fact, research shows that only 10% of our overall happiness depends on external things, such as the trappings of wealth, whereas 90% depends on our internal environment. Things like how relaxed we're feeling, how confident we feel, how peaceful.

- A laugh with a friend.
- A feeling of accomplishment after finishing a task.
- A quiet morning coffee where we feel fully at peace.
- The warmth of connection when someone truly listens to us.

These moments stack up to create resilience, joy and emotional well-being.

THE BOOZE ELEVATOR

When Janey Lee Grace (Well-being Coach and author) came on to the podcast, we discussed how we rarely notice the moment when drinking stops being something we do for joy and starts being something we do out of habit, or to escape. The shift is subtle, slow and easy to miss, but don't be fooled: alcohol only ever takes your levels of happiness in one direction.

Imagine stepping into an elevator. You're still in your early drinking years at this point, and you press the button, expecting to go up, to a place of fun, relaxation and happiness. After all, that's what you've been told alcohol will do for you. The doors slide shut, and the ride begins. You feel warm, carefree, maybe even invincible.

But hold on. You thought this ride was going to take you up, but this elevator seems to be going down. It's almost imperceptible at first. You don't realise it because the floor numbers aren't marked, and everyone around you seems to be enjoying the ride. But over time, as your drinking increases, you realise you are descending – floor by floor. Not that you let it worry you unduly…

Basement 1: The Anxiety Floor
The first signs are easy to dismiss – a creeping restlessness, a vague sense of unease. But beneath the surface, your brain is already compensating as, when the alcohol wears off, your nervous system ramps up stress hormones like cortisol to counteract its depressant effects. Over time, you begin to notice a cycle: feeling more on edge the day after drinking, and reaching for another drink to calm it. One round fuels the next – and the descent continues.

Basement 2: The Regret Floor

Now things start to chip away at your self-trust. You keep making promises to yourself – 'Just one', 'Not tonight', 'Only on weekends' – and breaking them. You send texts at 2am, let secrets slip that aren't yours to share. You have a nagging feeling that you're a little embarrassing; a little less in control than you'd like. It's not always about dramatic mistakes or blackouts. It's about a slow loss of confidence in your own boundaries. And the more regret builds, the more tempting it becomes to drink to silence the voice reminding you.

Basement 3: The Disconnection Floor

Alcohol was supposed to help you feel more like yourself – looser, freer, more open. And yet somehow not. Something is shifting. Your instincts are getting duller. Your inner compass is quietening. You stop checking in with how you really feel. Real emotions become harder to access. You mistake this numbness for relaxation. But really, you're further from yourself than ever. The connection that once felt enhanced has quietly faded.

Basement 4: The Shame Floor

At this point, drinking has become routine – not because it's fun, but because it's familiar. You're no longer choosing it; it's an automatic default. And though you try to downplay it – 'Everyone drinks', 'It's just my thing' – something inside you knows the truth. You're not at ease with your drinking any more. But facing that truth is hard. So the cycle continues. The elevator keeps going down.

Basement 5: The Hopelessness Floor

This is the lowest level. It doesn't happen overnight. Not a dramatic crash, but a slow erosion of one drink, one hangover, one broken promise at a time. You feel flat, uninspired. The spark is gone. You find yourself stuck in patterns you swore you'd change – not because you don't care, but because you feel worn down by it all. Your world gets smaller. Your confidence shrinks. Dreams you once had gather dust. You start making deals with yourself – 'I'll cut back next month', 'I'll just get Christmas out the way'. You keep hoping that alcohol will lift you, but deep down you know: it's only ever taken you lower.

The scariest thing about this metaphor is that everyone thinks they're on a different ride.

- The first-time drinker thinks they're just here for fun.
- The weekend warrior thinks they're in control.
- The moderate drinker thinks they're on safe ground.
- The heavy drinker doesn't realise how far they've already descended.

But when we realise the elevator only goes in one direction, we can stop hoping for a better ride – and start looking for a better way.

The loan shark

Let's end with another insight from Matt Phelan, who described alcohol as a happiness loan: something you borrow for the evening… but always end up having to pay back, with interest. Maybe it'll be later that evening. Maybe the next morning, but you'll eventually have to cough up.

I'd go as far as to say that alcohol is a loan shark. That night of fun didn't actually create joy. You just borrowed it from your future self, who will wake up paying for it in exhaustion and regret. Like a sneaky debt collector, alcohol always comes knocking for its payment. And the more you drink, the bigger your debt becomes.

Real happiness is not something we can borrow or loan. It's something we own, and have to tend and turn up for.

And that can only happen when we stop running and looking constantly to the future for that thing that keeps eluding us, and make ourselves present in the here and now.

Conversations feel richer. Moments feel more meaningful. And the best part? We actually get to remember them. Imagine waking up every day with a clear mind, no regrets and a deep sense of peace.

That's real happiness.

KEY TAKE-AWAYS:

- We credit alcohol for happiness it didn't create. Advertising and culture insert it into joyful scenes – and we mistake it for the cause.
- True happiness is internal. Research shows connection, meaning and presence drive well-being – all things alcohol quietly undermines.
- Alcohol is a downward spiral. The 'booze elevator' may start with a lift, but it often ends in anxiety, regret and disconnection.
- Happiness isn't something to chase. It comes when we remove the blockers – not when we keep adding more.
- Without alcohol, joy is real. Presence replaces regret, confidence builds and fulfilment stops coming from a bottle.

Food for thought:

1. **Have you ever mistaken the absence of negative emotions for happiness?**
   When you drink, are you truly happy or just less uncomfortable?

2. **Is alcohol quietly widening a happiness gap?**
   Is it separating you from the very things that make life meaningful?

3. **How far down have you gone on the booze elevator?**
   Have you ever started drinking thinking, 'This will be fun', only to feel anxious, regretful or disconnected later? Can you see how ultimately alcohol only has a 'Down' button?

4. **Can you name a time when you felt pure, unfiltered happiness – without alcohol?**
   Think about a childhood memory, a moment of connection, a time of deep purpose. What did it feel like? How is it different from an alcohol-induced high?

Relevant podcast episodes:

Episode 19. Alcohol-free Peace: Self-love, ADHD & Perimenopause

Episode 21. The Drivers of Happiness and the Influence of Alcohol

Episode 23. Measuring Your Personal Happiness

Episode 25. The Hidden Drivers of Behaviour and Addiction

Episode 31. From Grey Area Drinking to Holistic Health

Episode 39. From Alcohol to Authenticity

Episode 47. How do I Cope with Really Low Moments?

Episode 86. From Alcohol to Radical Integrity

PART 2

REFLECTION & VISION

CHAPTER 8

SEEING THE FULL PICTURE

At this point, we've explored how alcohol affects emotions, relationships and happiness. We've examined its hidden costs, its false promises, and the way it subtly takes up space in our lives. Now, it's time to make it personal, and turn the lens inwards.

Because this isn't just about alcohol. This is about you.

For so long, we've been taught to ask the wrong question: 'Is my drinking bad enough?'

It's the question we've been conditioned to ask by a society that normalises alcohol at every turn. As long as we're not messing with our relationships, failing upwards at work, or generally sabotaging our own life, we tell ourselves everything is fine. We compare our drinking to examples of 'other people's' behaviour at the extreme end of the spectrum – violence, public meltdowns, drink-driving offences – and as long as we don't see ourselves in those stories, we assume there's no real issue.

But that's a smokescreen. Because drinking doesn't have to be 'bad enough' to be holding you back.

The real question is far more important: 'Is my life good enough?' i.e. Is it the life you truly want? Are you the person you imagined becoming? Are you moving towards your goals, or have they become distant ideas – things you'll get to some day?

Because alcohol isn't just a habit. It's a keystone habit. One that quietly influences everything else. Your energy. Your confidence. Your sleep. Your relationships. Your sense of purpose.

So instead of asking whether your drinking is 'bad', ask this instead: 'Is alcohol helping me become the person I want to be?'

And if the answer is no, then maybe it's time for something to change.

DON'T JUST 'SETTLE'

The purpose of checking in on your relationship with alcohol is not to judge yourself. It's to be honest with yourself, and just make sure that drinking is truly adding to your life, rather than taking from it. That it's on your terms. That you're in the driving seat, 100% enjoying the ride, and not just going along with it out of habit.

A key part of this is zooming out and asking: 'Is alcohol compromising me in ways I haven't even noticed?'

Because the cost of drinking isn't just measured in pounds, dollars, or the occasional rough morning. It's in the things we lose slowly, imperceptibly, over time.

Since I stopped drinking, my life has improved in every single dimension. Some of these improvements were predictable, given the depths I'd sunk to. But others? They caught me off-guard. It wasn't just my energy, sleep and mood that changed; it was my motivation, my cognitive sharpness, my relationships, my skin, my whole sense of self.

And that's when I realised something.

As drinkers, we settle.

We don't even know we're doing it, because the decline is so gradual. Sub-optimal sleep. Sub-optimal energy. Sub-optimal cognitive skills. Sub-optimal moods. Sub-optimal motivation. Sub-optimal relationships.

Not falling apart. Just... not thriving.

We may tell ourselves it's a trade-off worth making – that the pleasure of drinking is worth the price we pay. But more often, we simply don't see it.

THE BOILING FROG EFFECT

If social conditioning had kept me from questioning my drinking, my tendency to write off discomfort as 'just part of life' kept me there even longer.

I blamed my exhaustion in my 30s on having young kids. The aches and pains in my 40s? Well, I'm not as young as I used to be. The creeping weight gain? Classic midlife. The mood swings and emotional lows? Obviously, perimenopause.

Except they weren't. Or maybe they were a bit, but it certainly wasn't the full picture.

I was the frog in the Boiling Frog Tale. The one that

doesn't realise it's in danger until it's too late.

The story goes like this:

If you drop a frog into a pot of boiling water, it will immediately jump out to save itself. But if you place that same frog in lukewarm water and slowly turn up the heat, it won't perceive the gradual rise in temperature as a threat. Instead, it adapts; adjusting, tolerating, convincing itself that everything is still fine. By the time it finally realises something is wrong, it's already too weak to escape.

The moral? When dysfunction creeps in slowly, we normalise it. We adapt to a life that is less than it could be.

And that's exactly how alcohol works.

It doesn't rob us overnight. It takes little pieces, bit by bit. Until one day, we look back and realise how much has been lost.

For me, when I finally confronted the truth about my 'harmless' habit, one thing became inescapably clear: alcohol was compromising every facet of my life.

Now, I know not everyone finds themselves in that place. You might not be drinking daily or experiencing dramatic fallout – but even moderate drinking can sometimes be the thing quietly dulling your shine.

The point is that you don't have to have 'a problem' with alcohol for it to be standing in the way of something better. You might even be sitting there thinking that your life is pretty damn good… but what if it could be great?

If alcohol is the reason for even one sub-optimal facet in your life, then it might be the very thing holding you back from moving from good to great.

And wouldn't that be a shame?

Because after all, we only get one shot at this life.

THE POWER OF KNOWING YOUR 10/10

Let me share a story.

Many years ago, early in my career, I was in the process of changing jobs when I was offered a session with a career coach. It was my first experience of coaching. I wasn't sure what to expect, but it was free, so I figured, 'Why not?'

After some polite chit-chat over a plate of Hob-Nobs, the coach asked me what I thought was a very straightforward question: 'On a scale of 1 to 10, how satisfied were you in the job you're leaving?'

Without hesitation, I answered 7/10.

It felt like the right number. I wasn't miserable, but I knew there was room for improvement. I was leaving my current role for a reason. The job hadn't given me everything I wanted, but neither had it been a disaster. A solid seven.

I was feeling pretty pleased with myself, mentally patting myself on the back for such a balanced, considered response… until she hit me with her next question: 'So what does 10/10 look like?'

Bugger me. I didn't have a clue.

She had me. Completely stumped. I had no idea what a 10/10 job looked like, because I'd never actually thought about it.

She smiled knowingly. 'Interesting,' she said. 'Because if

you don't know what 10/10 looks like, how do you know you're at a seven?'

Don't you just hate smart people?

Her message was simple but profound: if you don't have a clear sense of what 'ideal' looks like, how can you accurately measure where you are?

She had been talking about my career, but the same principle applies to every area of life – our health, our relationships, our sense of purpose, our happiness.

And this is exactly what I'm inviting you to do next.

There's a powerful coaching tool that helps make the abstract more tangible. It's called the Wheel of Life because a) it's round, and b) it's divided into sections, with each 'spoke' representing a different aspect of a well-balanced life.

This next exercise isn't about alcohol – it's about you. And it's a pivotal moment for radical honesty, as you ask yourself what you are really thirsty for – and for thinking deeply about the life that you want. So please do not skim over this, but instead grab a pen and paper – because in working through this exercise you will reveal the bigger picture, and understand how every piece of your life connects.

It's about spotting the gaps and recognising where things might be out of balance. It's about getting clear on what 10/10 actually looks like for you – and creating a personal little contract with yourself, to intentionally shape the life you're craving.

THE WHEEL OF LIFE

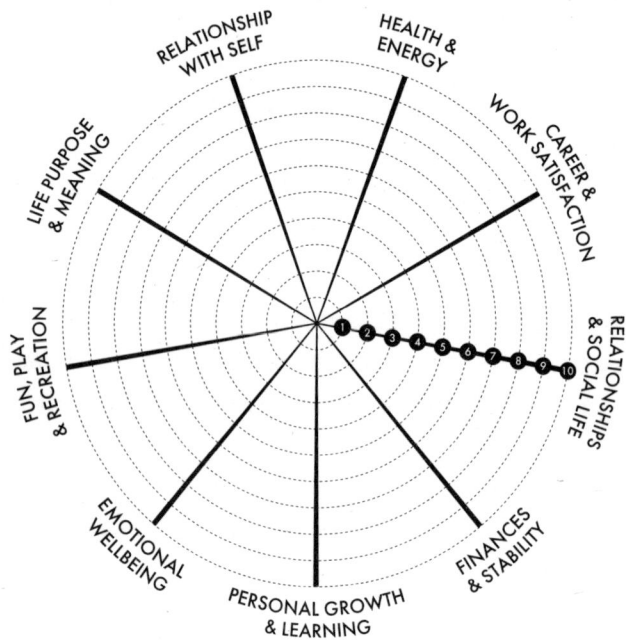

The spokes of a typical Wheel of Life include key areas such as:

- **Health & energy** – Do you feel physically strong, well-rested and energised?
- **Career & work satisfaction** – Are you fulfilled in what you do? Does it align with your values?
- **Relationships & social life** – Do you have deep, meaningful connections?
- **Finances & stability** – Are you financially stable and in control?

- **Personal growth & learning** – Are you evolving, learning and expanding?
- **Emotional wellbeing** – Do you feel mentally resilient, balanced and at peace?
- **Fun, play & recreation** – Are you experiencing genuine joy, play and creativity?
- **Life purpose & meaning** – Do you feel connected to something bigger than yourself?

These categories make sense intuitively, at first glance, but you'll find it gets much more interesting when you actually sit down and rate yourself in each area. That's when the gaps start to emerge.

And I'm adding one more essential spoke – one that, in truth, affects every single other area on the wheel.

THE 9TH SPOKE

If there's one relationship that shapes your life more than any other, it's the one you have with yourself. As Laura Bartlett put it, when she came on to the podcast: 'I used to care way too much about what others thought of me... Yet I'm the one who has to be with me every single day. So I have to make sure that *I* like me and *I* love me.'

She's right. You might see your friends occasionally. Your partner, more often. But you are with yourself 24/7.

And yet, how often do you actually check in on this relationship? The way you see yourself, the way you speak to yourself, how much you trust yourself. All of this influences every single other area of your life.

It affects the way you show up in relationships.

It determines how you treat your body and mind.

It shapes the decisions you make, and whether they serve you or sabotage you.

And here's where alcohol comes in. If drinking is making you feel disconnected, regretful or not in control, then it's harming your relationship with yourself. Full stop.

MY TRUTHS

Alcohol cost me much more than money. It chipped away at every dimension of my life. Some that were glaringly obvious, and others in ways so insidious that I only saw them clearly when I stopped drinking.

Emotional well-being
It's fair to say I was not a happy bunny. Alcohol had become a source of constant inner turmoil; a daily battle of wills between the intellectual part of me that didn't want to drink and the emotional part that believed I needed it. It was exhausting.

I lived in a permanent state of anxiety and stress. Mornings were filled with regret, nights with restless overthinking. And the realisation that I was not in control of my drinking was devastating to my self-esteem.

I had always seen myself as capable, intelligent and driven.

But this? This made me feel weak. Every time I said I wouldn't drink but did, my confidence in myself eroded a little more.

Health and energy

Where do I start with this one? I was carrying extra weight, my body was starting to ache, and my energy levels were permanently low.

Every morning, I started the day on the back foot, with a fuzzy head, sluggish body and compromised sleep, making even the idea of exercise feel impossible. Sure, there were token efforts (a cycle ride here, a yoga class there) but they only reinforced just how far from optimal health I really was.

And then, there was menopause creeping up on me – something I hadn't fully appreciated until I spoke to Lauren Chiren on the podcast. She described how the symptoms of perimenopause, i.e. brain fog, mood swings, poor sleep, are eerily similar to the effects of alcohol. And I realised I had been pouring fuel on the fire. Alcohol wasn't helping me unwind; it was making everything ten times worse.

Relationships and social life

Alcohol creates friction. It makes you more erratic, less patient, and situations more volatile. And for me, it involved an element of secrecy that corroded trust over time. There were arguments with my husband that didn't need to happen. He never quite knew which version of me would walk through the door. He was always braced, always vigilant, scanning for signs I'd gone too far. That kind of tension is a slow leak in any relationship. There were mornings lost to hangovers when I wasn't fully present for my kids. There were friends I drifted away from, because my world revolved around drinking and, if theirs didn't, we had less and less in common.

It also shaped the kinds of friendship I sought out. I gravitated towards people who drank like I did – because they helped normalise my habits. Drinking became the glue, even if the bond itself was thin. Looking back, some of those relationships weren't rooted in real intimacy, but in mutual permission to keep going.

I used to think alcohol helped me connect – and yes, it brought people together, loosened me up, made me feel sociable. But the question is: what kind of connection was I really experiencing?

Amber Hollingsworth, a therapist who works with families affected by alcohol, put it plainly: 'Alcohol doesn't help you connect with those around you. It helps you check out.'

This struck a chord. Because when I think back to the nights out, the boozy dinners, the parties and holidays – there were fun moments, sure. But was I really present? Often, I was more in my own head. More reactive. More focused on managing my emotional state than tuning in to others. If everyone's numbing at the same time, are we really connecting – or are we just coexisting, mistaking shared disconnection for closeness?

Ironically, I was reaching for alcohol to feel more connected, but ended up more distant. And the most painful realisation was that this also applied to my relationship with my children. Plus, what was I teaching them? I wanted them to grow up seeing a mum who was strong, in control, present. Instead, they saw a mum who needed wine to cope. Kids don't miss a thing. They see see everything – the wine glass in your hand, the way your mood shifts, the way you joke about needing a drink. And as much as I loved them fiercely, I couldn't deny that alcohol was stealing moments from us.

Finances and stability

Alcohol is expensive. I had never actually sat down and worked out how much I was spending, but when I did, it was horrifying. A bottle of wine (or two) most nights, rounds at the bar, wine with meals out. It adds up very quickly. A rough back-of a-fag-packet calculation showed that alcohol had cost me tens of thousands of pounds over the years. I kid you not! Here it is:

- A very conservative £10 a day, for the last 30 years = £70 per week × 52 weeks of the year × 30 years = £109,200.
- Then there were the occasions when I'd 'go large' – holidays, Christmas, birthdays, etc. So add in an extra (but still conservative) £70 a week for 4 weeks each year = 70 × 4 × 30 = £8,400.
- So, that's nearly £120,000 spent just on booze over the last 30 years, i.e. £4,000/year. And then there were the taxi fares home when driving wasn't an option, the impulsive take-aways, the lost items and the wasted gym memberships, etc. I could easily get to £150,000 in total, i.e. £5,000/year.

Sobering, isn't it? I look back now and consider how often I told myself I 'can't afford' the things that would have truly nourished me – the restorative holiday, the career-enhancing course, the health-boosting gym membership. I poured thousands down my neck without a second thought, while quietly shelving the things that might genuinely improve my life. Imagine what £150,000 could have done. Not just in material terms – but in enjoying a sense of freedom, energy and self-worth.

Fun, play and recreation

At first, drinking feels expansive – big nights out, exciting plans, spontaneous decisions. But over time? It becomes limiting. I stopped doing things I used to love. I never got round to visiting those galleries I used to enjoy, I didn't try new hobbies. I turned down activities that didn't involve drinking, or where I'd have to drive. Slowly, my world shrank until my definition of 'fun' was just… well, drinking.

Career and work satisfaction

I used to be driven, ambitious and focused. But alcohol quietly took chunks out of my best self at work. Lost mornings, sluggish thinking, missed opportunities. I had big ideas that never quite turned into action.

I wasn't falling apart. I was functioning. But I was functioning at half capacity and never quite firing on all cylinders. Over time my confidence took a hit. The feeling that I was clinging on by my fingertips, one misstep away from being found out, meant I played small. And the worst thing? I knew

I was capable of so much more and I was pissing away my potential.

Personal growth and learning
I always wanted to read more, learn more, expand my mind, but drinking had a way of stealing time. I'd make big plans – but then I'd have a drink. And the drink would make me tired. And suddenly, my plans to learn Spanish, take a course, or write that blog post would vanish into a fog of tomorrow, tomorrow, tomorrow. Looking back now, I realise that my curiosity and interest in life was waning. And of course, with addiction, comes the most stagnating of thoughts: 'This is who I am… and how things will always be'.

Life purpose and meaning
Deep down, I was avoiding something. As we highlighted in chapter 7, alcohol keeps us from asking bigger questions, like whether we are truly fulfilled. For me, it pleasantly numbed the existential itch, and the whispers of discontent that might have pushed me to make big, bold changes. Only when I stopped drinking, did I: a) start to ask what I really wanted from life, and b) have the wherewithal to actually hear, and listen to, the answer.

My relationship with myself
This 9th spoke did indeed prove to be the biggest one. I was disappointed in myself every single day. I was letting myself down, and I knew it. I was letting other people down, particularly my kids, and I knew it. I was hiding my drinking, and

therefore not living an honest, proud life. I hated looking in the mirror. The erosion of self-trust had leaked into everything – my confidence, my decision-making and my very self-worth.

NOW IT'S YOUR TURN

Grab that pen and use the Wheel of Life template to take a radically honest snapshot of where you are today.

Step 1: Score your life
- Take the centre of the wheel as 1 (low satisfaction) and the outer edge as 10 (high satisfaction).
- Score each area by placing a dot on your ranking.
- Now go round and join the dots on each spoke – this shape represents your life today.

Step 2: Reflect on your wheel
- How do you feel when you look at it?
- Which areas feel strong? Which feel neglected?
- Which areas are of greatest importance to you?
- How are you currently spending your time and energy in these areas?

Step 3: Define your 10/10 life
- Focusing on the areas most important to you, what does 10/10 look like? Forget where you are now, and just think big.

- What would fully thriving in these areas feel like?
- If the specifics are unclear, focus on your feelings e.g. what would make you feel more energised, purposeful, creative, free?

Step 4: Identify what's holding you back
- What's stopping you from reaching your 10/10 life?
- What habits, fears or beliefs are keeping you stuck?

Step 5: Consider the impact of alcohol
- To what degree is alcohol playing a role?
- If alcohol wasn't in the picture, would any of these scores improve?

That's it – you've just taken a powerful step. The clearer the picture, the easier it is to make meaningful, aligned change. Use this insight as your starting line.

Ask: where could a small shift make the biggest difference? What needs more of you – and what might need less?

Be bold. And remember: you don't have to overhaul your entire life to feel better. You just have to stop settling for one that's out of sync with who you really are – and who you want to be.

THE BIG DOMINO

Picture a line of dominos. You know exactly what happens when the first one tips: a tiny push sets off a chain reaction, one piece knocking over the next, building momentum until everything falls.

This is the premise of 'The Big Domino', a concept popularised by Gary Keller in his bestselling book, *The One Thing*. His point is that if you want to make a massive change in your life, don't try to fix everything at once. Instead, identify the one single thing that, if you changed it, would make everything else easier or irrelevant.

If you can tip the right domino, the rest will follow.

Most people don't think of alcohol as a Big Domino. They think of it as a small indulgence. A harmless habit, a social pastime, a way to unwind. But if you step back and look at the bigger picture, you start to see the reality.

Alcohol weaves its way through everything. It affects your health. Your energy. Your career. Your relationships. Your self-esteem. Your sense of purpose.

If alcohol is compromising multiple areas of life, then changing your relationship with it is one of the most powerful moves you can make.

It's THE thing. Topple this one domino, and everything else starts to shift.

Here's how it played out for me

The moment I knocked over the Big Domino, everything changed.

- My energy skyrocketed. I woke up feeling rested, clear-headed and ready for the day. No more mental fog, no more sluggishness, or feeling like I just had to push

through. Both my mental and physical health improved dramatically. My anxiety levels dropped, leading to better sleep and a more balanced nervous system.
- Better sleep (the root of so much), better diet and more exercise all contributed to weight loss. And over time, I noticed a quiet robustness returning – in my body, yes, but also in my mind. I felt steadier. Less reactive. More resilient. The little things didn't throw me off course so easily. I had a growing sense of trust in myself – not just to get through the day, but to make the most of each one.
- My confidence returned. Actually, scrub that. My confidence skyrocketed. I had beaten something that had truly been holding me back. So I felt invincible and capable of anything. Plus, no more second-guessing myself, no more inner critic, fuelled by regret. I felt in control of my choices and my future.
- I stopped feeling like I was constantly failing. The endless cycle of 'I'll do better tomorrow' was gone. Instead of guilt and frustration, I felt free.
- My relationships deepened. I wasn't just physically present with my kids, I was also, critically, emotionally present. I wasn't numbed or distracted. I was there, fully engaged, soaking up the moments. And my relationship with my husband grew stronger. It wasn't just that I wasn't hiding and retreating any more, which of course helped. It was more that he knew who was going to walk through the door. That I was going to show up as me. Imperfect certainly, but me.

- My ambition reignited. Without alcohol draining my time and headspace, I had my clarity, focus and drive back. With bells on, because I felt like I was making up for lost time. I suddenly had the energy and motivation to go after the things which for years I had been 'too tired' or 'too busy' for. What's more, I had the time back. I woke earlier and refreshed. In fact, I reckon I reclaimed about two hours a day, which is incredible considering just how frequently I whinged about not having enough hours to do everything on my plate.
- I began to explore the things I wanted to build into my life, knowing that I had the time, energy and money to do them. Piano lessons? Why not? A return to the Badminton court after a 35-year absence? Why not? Game on!

And the crazy thing is, I didn't lose a single thing. I didn't lose fun. I didn't lose connection. I didn't lose confidence. I didn't lose a single friend. I just gained more of everything I was actually searching for, nudging my life towards 10/10.

Now, this won't be everyone's story. You might not be drinking like I was drinking – but it's worth asking: what could change, even subtly, if it weren't in the picture?

When she came on to the podcast, Laura Bartlett summed it up perfectly. Just before quitting drinking, and having built an incredibly successful business, she asked herself: 'If I have been able to achieve all this while drinking... imagine what I could do if I didn't?'

The crux of it is this: going alcohol-free is a gateway, not a destination. Because here's the real gift of going alcohol-free: you're not just removing something. You're creating space to build a life you don't want to escape from.

A life where your needs are met – no numbing required.

Where joy isn't borrowed, but cultivated.

Where your days feel aligned with who you are, and your nights don't need erasing.

It's not about perfection. It's about possibility.

You start living in a way that feels more like you – with all your energy, creativity, confidence and connection intact. And from that place, the question becomes: what else becomes possible now?

KEY TAKE-AWAYS:

- We've been conditioned to ask the wrong question: 'Is my drinking bad enough?' Instead, we should ask: 'Is my life as good as it could be?'
- Alcohol is a keystone habit. It quietly influences everything, from energy and mood to confidence, purpose and relationships.
- The Wheel of Life exercise reveals how easy it is to settle when decline is gradual. Alcohol often steals from us in increments we don't notice... until we look back and realise how much we've lost.
- The most important relationship we have is the one we have with ourselves.
- Rethinking alcohol isn't about restriction. It's about expansion

– choosing one powerful change (your Big Domino) that triggers clarity, confidence and a ripple effect of transformation.

Relevant podcast episodes:

Episode 6. Raising the Bar Without Alcohol
Episode 7. Taking Charge
Episode 9. The Truth About Alcohol & Sleep
Episode 19. Alcohol-free Peace: Self-love, ADHD & Perimenopause
Episode 21. Key Drivers of Happiness and the Influence of Alcohol
Episode 31. From Grey Area Drinking to Holistic Health
Episode 34. From Alcohol to Authenticity
Episode 76. From Booze to Belief: Confidence without Alcohol

PART 3

PRACTICAL TOOLS & STRATEGIES

CHAPTER 9

WHY CHANGE FEELS HARD (AND HOW TO MAKE IT EASIER)

If you're starting to sense that something in your life could shift – even subtly – that's not a signal to panic. It's a signal to pay attention. Because as you'll know by now, awareness is the beginning of transformation.

Maybe you've seen that alcohol is your 'big domino', demanding of a rethink.

Maybe you've spotted something else during the Wheel of Life'exercise – a relationship, a habit, a job, a boundary you've been avoiding.

Whatever it is, change doesn't begin with a masterplan.

It begins with a whisper: could life feel better than this?

And bear in mind that even when the answer is yes, even when we're deeply ready for something new, it can still feel hard to take that first step.

Not because we're lazy, weak or broken – but because we're human.

Change isn't about logic.

If it were, we'd all make brilliant decisions and good choices instantly. We'd eat more healthily, exercise daily, quit drinking effortlessly and never procrastinate. Real change? It's emotional, psychological and deeply ingrained in our identity. And of course this incurs resistance.

Even when we want to change, there's often an invisible force holding us back; a weight, a hesitation, a voice in our ear saying, 'Maybe not today.'

Here's the thing, though, about resistance:

- It isn't proof that change is impossible.
- It's proof that change is unfamiliar.

I tend to think of it as a 'security system' for the status quo.

THE COMFORT OF FAMILIARITY

Think of your brain as a high-tech security system, designed to detect and defend against change. It scans for anything unfamiliar. It sounds the alarm the moment you try to step outside the usual routine. And ultimately it convinces you that staying put is safer than stepping into the unknown.

When you try to change a deeply ingrained habit, like drinking, your brain doesn't assess whether the change is good or bad. It just knows it's different. And different, to the primal brain, often means danger.

That's why resistance shows up. It's like an overprotective bodyguard standing at the door of your comfort zone. The moment you attempt to leave, it steps in front of you:

- 'Whoa! This is unfamiliar. Are you sure?'

- 'This feels uncomfortable! Let's just stay where it's easy.'
- 'What if you fail? What if it's worse on the other side?'

This is not a sign that you're incapable of change. It's just your brain doing what it's designed to do – which is keep you in the familiar, because familiar feels safe.

Have you ever stayed in a bad relationship longer than you should have? Or stuck with a job you hated, even though you knew you could do better?

That's resistance at work.

In my case, the familiarity of my day-to-day drinking was something I desperately wanted to escape. But it took me a long time to be able to make the break. The brain prefers familiarity over happiness. It would rather keep you in a predictable but unsatisfying situation than take the risk of something new. This is why we:

- Stay in routines that drain us.
- Repeat habits we know aren't serving us.
- Sabotage ourselves when we're on the verge of something better.

Because even a painful pattern feels safer than stepping into the unknown.

Alot of people don't address drinking behaviours – either cutting down or quitting altogether – because these changes involve journeying into uncharted territory. Drinking might be all they've known for 20, 30, 40 years, and if they give it up, they will be opening up a whole new world that they don't know yet. And this to some people is scary.

They'd much rather stay in the comfort of knowing what drinking gives them – even if they've begun to work out that it's taking an awful lot away from them too.

I have described my experiences of alcohol dependency as feeling like I was stuck in a dark room, struggling to find the door. Unable to locate it, but also fearful that even if I could, I would be scared to open it and walk through it. Scared of what was on the other side and the world that awaited me. Oh my god, did I hate that room. But regardless of that, staying there was at least a known entity. The other side of the door was terrifying. A world I didn't know how to navigate, and didn't think I'd be able to cope with. Ultimately I didn't know who I would be. I had never met the non-drinking version of me – and, given my lack of tools at the time, I did not see that new person flourishing in such a totally alien landscape.

THE POWER OF IDENTITY

Resistance to change doesn't just come from the brain's love of familiarity. It's also about identity. Who we think we are. Who others believe us to be. And what it means to step away from all of that.

I have had the opportunity to record a couple of podcast episodes with Dave Wilson (aka Sober Dave). For years, Dave wasn't just someone who drank. He was 'Glugs'. The guy who could drink anyone under the table. The one who walked into the pub to cheers and applause. It was the defining feature of how people saw him, and how he saw himself.

And when drinking becomes intertwined with our identity to this extent, the thought of change isn't just about habits. It's about self-definition. If I'm not the drinker, then who am I?

Many people stay stuck in their drinking patterns not because they love alcohol, but because they don't know what life looks like without it. If drinking is part of every social event, every celebration, every stress relief, then the idea of stepping away can feel like losing a part of yourself.

This is why breaking habits and dependencies from alcohol isn't just about behaviour change. It's about reinvention.

As I discussed with speaker and communication strategist Helen Packham, the stories we tell ourselves about who we are become powerful drivers of our choices.

Helen shared how deeply her own identity had become tied to drinking – not just as something she did, but as someone she was: the fun one, the party girl, the DJ. Letting go of alcohol meant facing the question: who am I without this?

And that's something many of us wrestle with. Not consciously, perhaps. But in the background, we're running the same silent script: I need alcohol to be confident, interesting, fun. I'm more myself when I drink.

Of course, these are just stories. Stories we've learned, often through repetition, advertising and cultural reinforcement. And as Helen put it so powerfully, 'Language isn't just about behaviour – it shapes our very sense of self.'

We need to learn how to change the words we use to describe ourselves, and so create space for a new identity to emerge.

For Dave, the shift didn't happen overnight. First, he had to stop drinking; then he had to rediscover who he was beyond the booze. And that took time. It meant replacing Glugs with someone new. Someone healthier, more present, more authentic.

This is why so many people struggle with changing their drinking behaviour. It involves accepting the loss of an old identity before the new one fully emerges. And this is more doable than you think: the truth is that identity is not a fixed label. You have rewritten yours before, countless times, as you've grown and evolved in life. You are no longer the same person now as you were when you were 15, or 25. You have changed. And you can do it again.

So the question isn't just: can I change my drinking behaviour? Or can I stop drinking? It's actually: 'Who do I want to become?'

THE FEAR OF LOSS VS THE REALITY OF MORE

Humans are wired to focus more on what they might lose than what they stand to gain. It's just the way we are. It's not a personal quirk, it's a well-documented psychological principle called 'loss aversion'. Studies show that people feel the pain of losing something twice as strongly as they feel the joy of gaining something equivalent.

And that's why, when faced with the idea of drinking less (or not at all), your brain instantly jumps to:

- But what about nights out with friends?
- What if I feel awkward at parties?
- How will I unwind without my glass of wine?

Your mind becomes laser-focused on what you think you're giving up, completely overlooking everything you stand to gain. This is how we get stuck – not just with drinking, but in many areas of life.

Imagine you're on a long hike, and you've been carrying a heavy rucksack. You've packed it full of things you thought you needed. But over the hours, the straps have cut into your shoulders, the weight has slowed you down, and you're starting to struggle.

Now, someone offers you the chance to take it off. To walk freely, to breathe deeply, to feel light for the first time in hours. Instead of unbuckling it, however, you hesitate. What if you need what's inside? What if you will regret letting it go?

So, you keep trudging forwards, carrying the weight, because even though it's uncomfortable and exhausting, you worry it's of value. There'll be stuff in there you can't do without.

This is exactly what happens with alcohol. We cling to it because we assume it's valuable. When really, it's just what we know. We don't realise how much lighter, freer and happier we'd feel without it.

WE'RE OUT OF PRACTICE

Think back to when you were a child. Growth was effortless. Actually, it was automatic. It wasn't something you had to work at. It just happened.

- Physically, you grew taller.
- Mentally, you were learning constantly – watching, listening, problem-solving, absorbing the world around you.
- Emotionally, you were adapting, evolving and figuring out who you were.

But at some point, that natural momentum stopped.

For most people, the last structured phase of growth ends in their early twenties. School is over. Maybe university. There are those first few years of figuring out a career. But then, unless you have professional qualifications to keep up with, life settles into routine. The brain stops being stretched. Learning slows down. Curiosity dims. We get comfortable.

And without even realising it, we can stop growing.

The worst part? We don't even notice it happening. It's like a gradual dimming of a light. One day, we wake up and wonder: 'Why does change feel so hard?'

The answer is because we've got rusty.

Imagine what would happen if you stopped exercising for ten years.

Would running feel impossible? Yes. Would lifting weights be uncomfortable? Of course. Would it mean you're incapable of getting strong again? Not at all. The discomfort isn't proof that you can't do it. It's proof that you just haven't in a while.

And growth (whether it's emotional, mental or behavioural) is the same. The reason change feels so scary isn't because you're incapable. It's because you haven't been flexing your growth muscles for a long time.

But muscles can be strengthened again. And the more you practise change, the easier it becomes.

If you live to be aged 90, and you're reading this aged 40, you still have more than half of your life ahead of you. Obviously, you can do the maths: if you're aged 50, that's still 40 years of possibility.

So why do we let personal growth end prematurely?

If you stopped to think about it, would you accept zero growth for the next 40 years? Would you be okay with the idea of repeating the same year, over and over, until you die? That's not a life. It's habitual existence.

Yes, change feels hard. Yes, growth is uncomfortable at first. But not because you can't do it. You're likely just out of practice.

And the good news? You can get back in the game. You can start again. You simply have to give yourself permission.

I am just about old enough to remember the cartoon character Popeye, a rough, tough, spinach-loving sailor. His catchphrase was: 'I yam what I yam and that's all that I yam.' It was his way of embracing his identity – unapologetic, unchanging and fiercely self-reliant.

What a fucking cop-out. It's a phrase we use when we've stopped believing we can change:

- I'm just someone who drinks – that's who I am.
- I've always been this way. It's just how I'm wired.
- I can't change now. It's too late.
- I'm from a family of big drinkers. It's my fate.

The idea that we are fixed, unchanging and incapable of growth isn't just limiting, it's scientifically wrong. The brain is adaptable. Identity is flexible. Who you are today is not who you have to be tomorrow.

Think about it. You are not the same person you were at 10, or 20, or even five years ago. Life has shaped you. Experiences have changed you.

We all have the ability to change – at any age, at any stage. The real question is: do you want to?

Because 'I am what I am' isn't the truth. It's just an excuse. And you deserve better than that.

SHIFTING OUR MINDSET

The good news is that a few simple mindset shifts can make change feel easier, natural and even exciting.

From 'missing out' to 'less is more'

Let's look a bit more closely at this idea that cutting back on alcohol will be a gain rather than a loss.

What if drinking less actually enhances everything?

This is the insight that broadcaster Adrian Chiles shared when he came on the podcast. For years, he had thought that moderation would ruin his social life. Instead, he discovered that drinking less meant enjoying alcohol more.

He became more mindful, savouring what he drank rather than mindlessly consuming it. His experiences became sharper, his connections more authentic, and he woke up feeling better instead of worse.

The truth is, the more we drink, the less we appreciate it. It becomes routine. Automatic. Something we do out of habit rather than something we truly enjoy.

Adrian provided some very simple advice: cut out the drinks you don't need, want or particularly enjoy. Similarly, Professor David Nutt advises that two drinks is often the tipping point – enough to enjoy the occasion without letting the night slide into something you later regret.

Both Adrian and David are highlighting the concept of diminishing marginal returns. The first drink is almost always the most pleasurable. The second still tends to be enjoyable. But beyond that, the value rapidly falls away. Additional drinks simply start to undo the benefits of the earlier ones, bringing tiredness, clumsiness and a loss of connection.

The truth is, if you tally up your weekly intake, a surprising number of units may come from drinks you didn't truly want or enjoy. Cutting them doesn't mean sacrificing pleasure – it means preserving it.

So, less isn't missing out. Less is being present for more.

From 'all or nothing' to 'small, consistent steps'

One of the biggest traps people fall into is all-or-nothing thinking. We convince ourselves that if we can't do something perfectly, there's no point in trying.

- If I can't quit drinking, why bother cutting back on it at all?
- If I am not likely to stick to exercising regularly, why even start?
- If I slip up once, I've failed.

But this mindset keeps us stuck. It makes change feel impossible before we've even begun.

The truth is that big changes aren't made in one dramatic leap. They are built through small, consistent actions.

- How do you eat an elephant? One bite at a time.
- Was Rome built in a day? No – but some of it was.

Instead of focusing on forever, focus on today. James Clear, author of *Atomic Habits*, and BJ Fogg, a Stanford behavioural scientist and author of *Tiny Habits*, both emphasise the power of tiny changes repeated over time. Because momentum matters more than perfection.

- Instead of thinking: 'I have to quit forever', think: 'I'm just not drinking today.'
- Instead of believing: 'I need to transform myself now', believe: 'I'm just making one better choice at a time.'

Perfection isn't the goal. Progress is.

Wait. Let's pause here. Because if you're anything like me – a recovering perfectionist raised in a world of instant results and grappling with a world of overnight makeovers – you'll be tempted to skip past this bit. You'll nod along politely, but secretly think, 'Yeah yeah, small steps, got it… now give me the real transformation.'

But this *is* the real transformation.

This is where it starts. This is the bit that matters most.

Because we don't change by overhauling our lives in one dramatic moment.

We change by showing up differently in a hundred tiny ones.

From 'fear' to 'excitement'

Most people assume that fear and excitement are opposites. That one is bad and the other is good. But the fascinating thing is that fear and excitement feel exactly the same in the body.

- Your heart beats faster.
- Your breath gets shallower.
- Your stomach flutters.
- Your senses sharpen.

The only difference is the story that your brain tells you about it.

- If you call it fear, your body reacts with panic.
- If you call it excitement, your body floods with anticipation.

That means you can flip the script. Instead of asking: 'What if this goes wrong?', you can instead ask: 'What if this is amazing?'

This 'what if?' shift is a really neat trick to turn anxiety into excitement.

Most fear is built on negative what ifs?:

- What if I fail?
- What if this is hard?
- What if I regret this?

But excitement is built on positive what ifs?:

- What if this is the best decision I ever make?
- What if my whole life changes for the better?

Both scenarios exist in the unknown. The only difference? The lens through which you choose to see them.

And here's another thing to remember: most of our fear-based 'what ifs?' rarely hold up under scrutiny.

- What if I look stupid?

- What if I mess up?
- What if people judge me?

Okay, but… so what?

Honestly – who's keeping score? Who really cares? And even if it does go a bit sideways… what's the worst that actually happens? You feel a bit uncomfortable? You learn something? You course-correct and carry on?

Sometimes the most liberating mindset shift is this. It's not that deep. Fear loves to inflate the stakes, but when you zoom out, most of the risks we dread are fleeting, forgettable and entirely survivable.

And once you realise that, the unknown starts to look a lot less scary – and a whole lot more exciting.

Let me give you a real example. I wanted to get back into badminton – partly for fitness, partly for fun, partly because I liked the idea of doing something that gave me a sense of progress, achievement and community. But straight away, the doubts kicked in: What if I'm not good enough? What if I make a fool of myself? What if everyone there is way better than me?

Still, I pushed past the nerves and turned up at a local club. And guess what? They told me I wasn't at quite the right standard.

Now, a few years ago, that might have felt humiliating. I might have gone home, embarrassed, and convinced myself never to try again. But this time I didn't spiral. I didn't catastrophise. I just thought: Well… I came, I tried. And now I know.

More importantly – and here's the part fear never predicts – one of the club members contacted me the next day. She put me in touch with a coach who was more aligned with my level. I started going to their sessions, rebuilt my confidence, and slowly, I got back in the game.

That experience could have been a rejection story. But it turned into a reconnection story. All because I gave it a go.

The next time fear kicks in, try this little exercise:

1. Acknowledge the feeling. 'My heart is racing. I've got butterflies in my stomach.'
2. Name it as excitement. Instead of saying: 'I'm nervous', say: 'I'm excited.'
3. Lean into the anticipation. Ask: 'What good things might be on the other side of this?'

This isn't fake positivity – it's science. Studies show that reframing anxiety as excitement increases performance, confidence and follow-through.

THE 4 C'S FORMULA

Most of us believe that to start something new we need to feel confident – to *feel ready*. That if we just wait long enough – until we feel braver, more certain, more capable – then we'll finally take action.

But that's not how growth works. Confidence isn't the prerequisite for change – it's the result of it.

Think about anything big you've ever done in life. Did you feel completely confident before you started? Or did confidence come *afterwards* – once you had proof that you could do it?

Dan Sullivan is an author and strategic coach, who came up with something called the 4 C's Formula as a way of plotting the real path to growth. It goes like this:

Step 1: Commitment

Before anything changes, you have to decide. You don't need to know *how* yet. You don't need to have a perfect plan. You just need to commit to the path, even if it feels uncertain.

This is the moment you say: *I don't have all the answers, but I'm doing this anyway.* It's the moment you stop waiting for confidence to appear and choose to act *in spite of* fear.

Step 2: Courage

Commitment is the spark, but courage is what carries you forwards.

Because the moment you decide to make a change, fear shows up. This is the moment most people turn back. They mistake fear for a stop sign, instead of what it really is: proof that you're stepping into something bigger.

Remember that every time you do something unfamiliar, your brain sends out an alarm: Danger! Unknown territory! But here's the thing: just because something is unfamiliar doesn't mean it's unsafe. You're not in danger. You're just growing.

Step 3: Capability

At first, you feel shaky. Uncertain. Like you're making it up as you go. But the more you *do*, the more capable you become.

For example:

- The first social event without drinking feels weird – then the second feels easier.
- The first stressful day without alcohol feels tough – then you prove to yourself you can handle it.
- The first few weeks might feel full of doubt – then one day, you realise you're actually enjoying your reduced-alcohol or alcohol-free life.

And suddenly, what once felt impossible becomes second nature.

Step 4: Confidence

Confidence is something you *build*. It's the by-product of action. You don't gain confidence by waiting. You gain confidence by *doing*. By stepping forwards, even when it's scary, and developing capability along the way.

So, if you've been waiting to feel ready before you make a change, stop waiting. You don't need confidence to start. You just need to start.

Commit first.

Courage will follow.

Capability will grow.

And before you know it, confidence will be something you own.

FEELING THE FEAR AND DOING IT ANYWAY

Susan Jeffers' iconic book *Feel the Fear and Do It Anyway* is based on a powerful truth: fear doesn't mean you can't do something. It just means you haven't done it YET.

Likewise, resistance: this isn't proof you're failing; it's proof that change is happening. It's not a wall, it's a doorway. And like any heavy door, the hardest part is the first push.

- At first, it barely moves. It takes effort, and part of you wonders if it's even worth it.
- But then, you push a little more, and it gives way.
- Once the door is open, you step into a whole new space.

This is how change works. The hardest part isn't building and maintaining new behaviours. The hardest part is getting past the first push of resistance. And once you do, you'll wonder why you waited so long.

Most people assume resistance means 'stop'. But resistance is actually a signpost telling you that you're standing at the edge of transformation. The stronger the resistance, the more important the change. If it wasn't worth it, your brain wouldn't fight so hard to keep you where you are.

This is why we coaches tend to spout stuff like: 'All change happens outside of the comfort zone.' If you wait until it feels easy, you'll be waiting forever. Instead, lean into the resistance. That's where the magic happens.

Think of your brain like a sat nav. It knows one route – the well-worn path of habit. Even if that path takes you through dodgy suburbs (like self-doubt, hangovers or regret), it's a route you've travelled so many times that it feels like the only way.

The moment you try to take a new road (towards drinking less, self-trust or growth), your sat nav throws a wobbly, telling you you've taken a wrong turn and urging you to let it direct you back on to the route you know. It's not guiding you based on what's *best* for you, it's just repeating old data. It assumes that because you've always gone this way, you should keep going this way. It doesn't yet know that there's a better, faster, kinder route ahead.

You don't need to erase fear. You just need to stop blindly following outdated directions. Trust yourself, keep moving forwards, and soon, your sat nav will catch up and recalibrate to your new, better direction of travel.

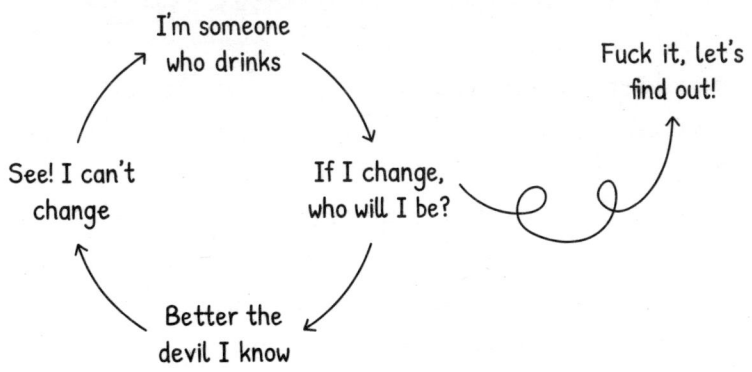

KEY TAKE-AWAYS:

- Resistance is a sign that change is happening. Your brain defaults to the familiar not because it's better, but because it feels safe.
- Identity can be rewritten. If drinking has been part of who you are, change may feel like loss – but identity is fluid, and you've evolved before.
- We fear loss more than we chase gain. This bias (loss aversion) keeps us stuck, even when there's far more to gain than lose.
- Discomfort doesn't mean you're doing it wrong. Change feels hard because you're out of practice – not because you're incapable.
- You don't need confidence to begin – only commitment. Action builds courage, and confidence follows.
- Fear and excitement are two sides of the same coin. Reframe the story: what if this is the best decision you'll ever make?

Food for thought: A powerful exercise in perspective

Up until now, we've explored awareness, we've looked at different perspectives and you've hopefully been doing oodles of reflection. Hopefully you've begun rethinking your relationship with alcohol and maybe even imagined what life could look like without it.

Now, it's time to feel it. Not just to think about change, but experience the weight of staying the same versus the freedom of making a shift.

Because when it comes to decisions that shape our lives, logic can only take us so far. Real change happens when we connect to our choices on an emotional level.

This exercise is designed to help you do exactly that.

So, take a deep breath. And let's take a journey into your future.

Scenario 1: The path of staying the same

- Step forward one year. Imagine yourself exactly as you are now, having chosen not to make any changes to your drinking behaviour. Maybe you told yourself: 'I'll deal with it later,' or maybe you convinced yourself that things were fine.
- Look at yourself in the mirror. How do you feel? Is there a sense of pride, or frustration? Do you feel energised and in control – or stuck in the same cycle?
- How does your body feel? Over the past year, how much alcohol has passed through it? Is there an impact on your energy, sleep or mental clarity?
- Look at your relationships. The people who care about you. Your partner, your kids, your closest friends. Do you feel more connected to them, or more distant? Have there been misunderstandings, missed moments, or times when alcohol came between you and the people you love?
- Now, travel three years into the future. Imagine three more years of this same cycle. You wake up and realise this is still where you are. You meant to make a change, but life kept rolling forward.

- Your body. Your mind. Your relationships. Your ambitions. Where are they now?
- Now, let's go even further. Ten years. A decade. What does life look like? Have things improved, or have they quietly eroded, little by little? What has been lost? Is this the future you want?

Pause here. Take a deep breath. Let that version of your future settle for a moment. Now, let's rewind, and consider a different path.

Scenario 2: The path of change

- Come back to today. You're standing at a crossroads. And this time, you choose differently.
- Now step forward a year. OK, so maybe it wasn't a perfect, linear journey. Maybe there were slip-ups. But over the past year, you made a real shift. Drinking is no longer the dominant force in your life.
- Look in the mirror. What do you see? Is there a different energy in your reflection? A spark that wasn't there before?
- How does your body feel? Is there a lightness? A sense of ease? Have you reclaimed the energy, sleep and clarity that alcohol once stole?
- Look at your relationships. Your kids, your partner, your friends. Are they seeing more of the real you? Do they trust you more? Do *you* trust yourself more?
- Now, go forward three years. Three years of being more present. More awake. More you.

- Now, go forward ten years. A decade of living without alcohol holding you back. What does this version of you look like? How do you carry yourself? What have you built, experienced and created?
- If you have children, imagine standing in front of them. What do they see? What do they admire? What kind of example have you set?
- Look back over the past ten years. How does change feel? Is it something you regret? Or does it feel like confidence?

Well done.

- Two paths. Two versions of you.
- One where nothing changes.
- One where everything opens up.

Relevant podcast episodes:

Episode 16. When Drinking is Part of Your Identity

Episode 43. How do I Cope with Setbacks?

Episode 50. Progress Over Perfection – A New Approach to Dry January

Episode 54. Breaking the Alcohol Cycle – Habits vs Dependency

Episode 55. Getting Unstuck

Episode 59. Practical Ways to Build Positive Habits

Episode 62. Our Alcohol Stories: Words that Can Change Your Life

Episode 63. How to Change Your Alcohol Stories

CHAPTER 10

REWIRING HABITS

WHY WILLPOWER DOESN'T WORK

Many people believe cutting back on alcohol (or building any better self-care habit, for that matter) is about willpower. But science shows willpower is unreliable.

This is so important, because it's the reason why most habit change fails. Or why attempts at alcohol-free breaks (like Dry January) are cut short, or end with binges and blow-outs.

What I mean by willpower is 'the use of conscious mental energy or effort to stop doing something or start doing something on a regular basis'.

So if you've ever tried to stop doing something regularly, like smoking, or biting your nails; or if you've tried to start doing anything regularly, like exercising and going to the gym – you'll likely have drawn on your 'willpower' and the principle of 'I'm going to do this, whatever it takes…'

In certain circumstances willpower can be helpful. And you may have to rely on it. Sometimes.

But it's not great if you're trying to effect long-term and sustainable change.

Why? Because willpower is a finite resource. In other words, it runs out.

Research shows that willpower is like a muscle or an energy reservoir. That is, you have a certain amount, but you soon use it all up. It's like watching the battery icon on your mobile phone dwindle over the course of a day. It drains and drains and when you get to the bottom, you have none left.

And the very act of exercising willpower drains and depletes us. So when we are faced with something challenging and hard, we have nothing left in the tank.

And this depletion of resistance brings on the 'fuck it effect'.

Not just 'fuck it... I'm going to have one'... but then also 'fuck it... I've already had one, so what the hell? I might as well just carry on.'

The point is that willpower is not the answer to long term behaviour change.

In fact, it can make things worse. Because if you are exercising your 'will' against alcohol, you're entering the language of combat. And if alcohol ends up 'winning', you can all too easily take away the message that you are not strong enough. Which is rubbish. You're just using the wrong weapon.

So if not willpower, then what?

Lasting change happens when you work with your brain's habit-forming system, not against it.

The good news here is that the same mechanisms that made alcohol an automatic habit can be hijacked to build better, healthier habits.

THE SCIENCE OF HABIT CHANGE

If you've ever tried to drink less and found yourself reaching for a glass of wine or a beer almost automatically, you're not alone. That's because drinking, like any habit, follows a predictable pattern in the brain. Understanding how this works is the key to changing your relationship with alcohol.

In his book *Atomic Habits*, James Clear describes how habits are formed.

He calls it the habit loop. Every habit, including drinking, follows a four-step cycle in the brain. This cycle happens on repeat, often without us even realising it:

1. The Cue → The trigger that starts the habit.
    - ◊ This could be a time of day (6pm), a place (the pub), an emotion (stress or boredom), or a social event (a party or dinner).
    - ◊ Your brain picks up on patterns, and when it sees a cue, it expects the habit to follow.

2. The Craving → The desire or urge to drink.
   This isn't a craving for alcohol itself – it's a craving for what alcohol represents:
    - ◊ Relaxation after a long day/Feeling included in a group/A quick way to numb an emotion.
    - ◊ Your brain isn't screaming 'I need alcohol!' – it's saying: 'I need relief, connection or distraction.'

3. The Response → The actual action: pouring the drink.
   - ◊ Because alcohol is the fastest, easiest way to get the reward, we reach for it automatically.
   - ◊ This is why drinking feels effortless – it's just the action that follows the craving.

4. The Reward → The feeling that reinforces the habit.
   - ◊ After drinking, you feel different: relaxed/more confident/disconnected from stress.
   - ◊ Your brain remembers this outcome and associates the cue with the reward. The more often this loop repeats, the stronger the habit becomes.

So here's the thing: the key to habit change isn't eliminating cravings. It's reprogramming the response to the same cue.

Instead of fighting against your brain's wiring, you need to change what happens between the craving and the action.

This is where small, strategic changes can start to shift the pattern – especially in the heat of the moment, when a craving sneaks up quietly, mid-scroll, mid-stress, mid-boredom.

And your brain pipes up with that familiar suggestion: 'You know what would help? A drink.'

It can feel like there's no substitute. No equivalent. No alternative that quite hits the same note.

But take a breath.

That craving?

It's not about the alcohol.

It's about what alcohol promises.

You don't crave the drink itself. You crave what you think the drink will deliver. This is such an important point to grasp. You think alcohol is going to provide:

Relief
Escape
Confidence
Connection
Permission to switch off

It's like your brain has followed a well-worn shortcut: Discomfort + Drink = Solution.

But here's the shift: what if, instead of shutting it down or giving in, you paused to ask, 'What am I really craving right now?'

Because so often, the drink is just a placeholder. A symbol. A learned response. Maybe what you actually want is…

- To be seen without having to perform
- To feel safe in your own skin
- To press pause on the noise in your head
- To let go – without guilt, without consequence

That craving is real. In fact, it's wise, because it's trying to help you meet a need.

But alcohol? That's just an old script. The autopilot.

So here's your invitation: if what you're truly craving is comfort, ease, freedom – what else might meet you there? Could it be lighting a candle and calling someone who gets you? A playlist that shifts your mood? Stepping outside to breathe deeply? Curling up in your softest clothes with zero expectations?

You're not denying yourself anything. You're just looking through a wider lens at what might give you what you need.

Yes, this takes practice, because emotional cravings don't respond well to logic – but they do respond to curiosity, to kindness, and to interrupting the pattern just long enough to try something new.

So, you're not just breaking a habit. You're building a new relationship – with your needs, your emotions and your power to respond differently.

And the more you do that?

The more space there is between craving and action.

And the more space there is – the more choice you have.

The Tiny Habits method

In his book *Tiny Habits*, B.J. Fogg suggests that the secret to habit change is in making it too easy to fail.

Most people fail at habit change, he says, because they try to go big overnight. They set rules like: 'I won't drink this week' or 'I'll quit alcohol forever' – only to feel overwhelmed, slip up and give up on the idea entirely. Big, sudden changes trigger resistance. Whereas tiny, effortless changes build momentum.

Instead of saying: 'I'll stop drinking at night', try something tiny and doable like:

- I'll have a thirst-quenching glass of water first

- I'll enjoy a tasty non-alcoholic drink before my usual first drink
- I'll just wait an hour longer before pouring a drink
- I'll swap my large wine glass for a smaller one (studies show this automatically reduces consumption)
- I'll alternate drinks, following the rule that for every alcoholic drink, I'll have a glass of water or a soft drink (not only does this slow down consumption, it also keeps you hydrated and reduces hangovers).

These are all small shifts that don't seem like much. And they certainly don't deny you alcohol, but they chip away at the old habit loop and create a new pattern.

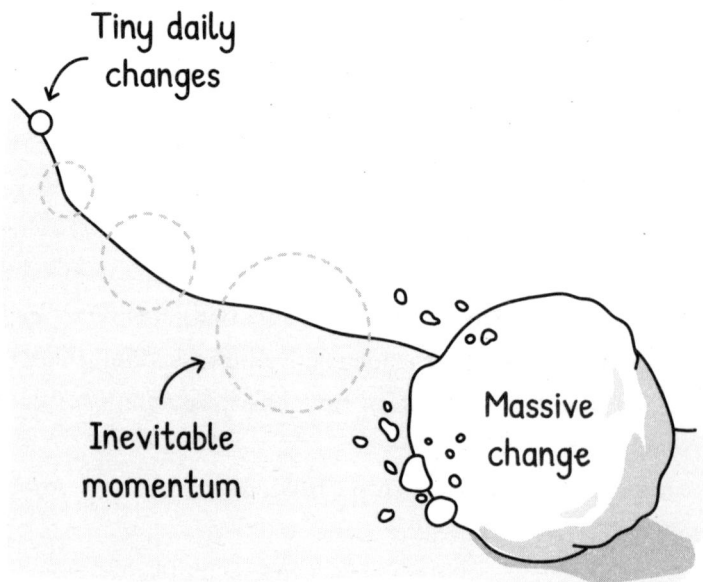

Fogg's point is that success isn't about the size of the action. It's about consistency. A tiny change done every day is more effective than a huge change you can't stick to. Over time, these small shifts retrain your brain, making drinking feel less automatic and giving you more control.

Think of it like nudging a steering wheel just a few degrees. You're not going to veer off immediately, but over time those tiny adjustments will take you in a new direction.

THE POWER OF 'MAKING IT HARDER'

We often think of habit change as adding new behaviours, but one of the easiest ways to drink less is to make drinking less convenient. Behavioural science tells us that if something is easy, we'll do it more. If it's harder, we'll do it less. It's obvious really.

One of the biggest reasons we drink is simply because it's easy. The wine is right there. The beer is already in the fridge. The pub is on the way home. The glass is poured before we've even thought about it.

Bad habits thrive in frictionless environments. We drink because it's automatic, available and effortless. The trick is to introduce just enough friction to break the autopilot cycle.

Here's how you can make drinking less convenient, without banning yourself from it completely:

- Change your environment – make alcohol harder to reach. Move bottles to a high shelf, out of sight, or even

into the garage. The harder it is to grab, the more you'll pause and rethink.
- If you have wine and beer in the house, don't keep them in the fridge. When warm, these drinks are way less appealing, and the pause enforced by having to consider chilling them creates the friction that can prompt reconsideration.
- Don't buy in bulk – this sounds obvious, but if there's less alcohol at home, you'll naturally drink less:
  ◊ Certainly don't subscribe to wine clubs, where new deliveries turn up routinely and create a feeling of abundance.
  ◊ Don't include alcohol in the weekly shop, where again it is too easy just to scoop it into the trolley (be that in the supermarket or online).
  ◊ Instead, only buy it when you want it – enforcing a journey to the shop between wanting it and having it available.
- Introduce an interruption – if you usually drink at 7pm, set an alarm for 6.45pm, to ask yourself: 'Do I actually want this drink, or am I just following a routine?' Even a 10-second pause creates space for choice.
- Change the ritual – pouring a drink into a different type of glass, one you don't associate with alcohol, forces a tiny moment of awareness and interrupts an otherwise mindless action.

You don't have to eliminate alcohol overnight, or completely. Just introduce speed bumps that make drinking less automatic and more intentional. Every second of added friction is another opportunity to choose differently.

Think of it like putting your phone in another room when you don't want to scroll. Obviously, it doesn't stop you if you really want it, but it gives you just enough space to decide if it is what you really want in that moment. And that space? That's where change begins.

BUILDING BETTER HABITS FOR SELF-CARE

Looking after the solid self-care principles of nutrition, hydration, movement and sleep can stop that evening depletion and the feeling of lack/need.

On the podcast, Christopher Richards, founder of Atomic Growth and an expert in psychology and human behaviour, mentioned that habits that give us easy rewards, such as alcohol, sweet foods, scrolling on social media, can only really be broken when you have *already* replaced them. I consider greater self-care to be a huge part of this.

Building better habits specifically for self-care is important. And here's how it can be done: Step 1: Identify what alcohol was doing for you. Was it relaxation? Social comfort? Stress relief? Reward? Step 2: Find a replacement habit that meets the same need, in a better way.

For relaxation → Create a new wind-down habit
- Tiny Habit Starter: 'After I sit down at 7pm, I will take three deep breaths before deciding what to drink.'

- ◊ Swap the drink for a new sensory ritual: herbal tea, sparkling water in a wine glass, or a hot bath.
- ◊ Pair it with something enjoyable: a podcast, stretching, lighting a candle.

For stress relief → Quick stress-reset habits

- Tiny Habit Starter: 'After I feel stress rise, I will try a two-minute reset before I consider drinking.'
  - ◊ Step outside, shake out tension, stretch, journal or simply breathe intentionally.

For social confidence → The comfort of non-alcoholic rituals

- Tiny Habit Starter: 'Before going out, I will remind myself that I am enough and I don't need alcohol to have a good time.'
  - ◊ Reframe discomfort as excitement – the physiological response is the same.
  - ◊ Create a signature non-alcoholic drink to order or bring to events.

For reward → Upgrade your treat system

- Tiny Habit Starter: 'After I finish work, I will take a moment to acknowledge what I did well today.'
  - ◊ Instead of rewarding yourself with a drink, reward yourself with something more lasting and satisfying, something that actually enhances your life – a great meal, a new experience, morning energy.

MAKING CHANGES STICK

1. The power of identity: becoming the person who...
We don't act according to what we want. We act according to who we believe we are.

Think about a smoker who is trying to quit. If they say: 'I'm trying to stop smoking', they still fundamentally see themselves as a smoker – someone who just happens to be struggling with quitting. But if they say: 'I'm not a smoker', they shift their identity. And once you shift your identity, your habits follow.

The same applies to drinking.

If you tell yourself: 'I'm trying to drink less', you're still identifying as a drinker who is making an effort not to indulge. But when you start saying: 'I'm someone who takes care of myself', you create a new self-image. One that doesn't rely on alcohol to define enjoyment, relaxation or social confidence. This again shows the huge impact of our words and the stories we tell ourselves, as per my conversation with Helen Packham: the fact that we change our self-perception – our very identity – by simply changing our language.

Think of your identity like a compass. It guides your actions without you even realising it. Every time you make an intentional choice, you cast a vote for the person you are becoming.

- Opt for a non-alcoholic alternative? You've just reinforced the identity of someone who is in control of their choices.
- Choose to go for a walk instead of going to the pub?

You've just made another deposit into the bank of self-respect.
- Wake up feeling clear-headed and energised? That's proof you're stepping into a new version of yourself.

Small wins reinforce identity shifts. Even just one day of choosing differently makes you more of that person. It's not about perfection. It's about consistency.

When you begin seeing yourself differently, it's no longer about giving something up. It's about aligning with the person you want to be.

2. The rule of self-compassion: there's no such thing as failure

This is one of my mantras. Since giving up alcohol I have found endless other places where I can apply this to my life. I have found huge freedom in accepting I am nothing but one almighty work in progress. Seeing every misstep simply as 'data' is the most liberating of principles, and it reinforces a spirit of curiosity and learning. Something not gone to plan? It's just a signal showing you what's not working and where to adjust. The goal isn't to be perfect – it's to keep learning and keep going.

Think of change like learning to ride a bike. The first time you tried, you wobbled, you tipped over, you scraped your knee, or (if you're me) you ended up in a ditch of stinging nettles. But you didn't say: 'Well, that's it – I'm just someone who can't ride a bike.' You got back on, adjusted your balance and tried again. And eventually, it became effortless.

Drinking less works the same way. Some nights will feel easy, others won't. Some days you'll sail through without even thinking about alcohol, and other days an old trigger will trip you up. This doesn't mean you've failed. It means you're learning.

Instead of beating yourself up, ask yourself:

- What was the cue? (Was I stressed? Lonely? Celebrating?)
- What was I feeling? (Was I tired? Bored? Looking for connection?)
- What could I do differently next time? (Could I take a walk, call a friend, or plan ahead?)

Imagine you're on a road trip and you take a wrong turn. You wouldn't throw your hands up and say: 'Well, I guess I live here now.' You'd turn around and find your way back to the right road. This journey is the same. A single detour doesn't mean you're lost. It's just part of the trip.

3. The 'Witching Hour': how to navigate early evening

If you're wondering where to begin with habit change, let me introduce you to the concept of the 'Witching Hour'. The time of day when your drinking habit is at its strongest.

For many, this falls between 6-8pm, i.e. the transition from day to evening. From work life to home life. From responsibility to relaxation. Maybe it starts when you walk through the door. Or maybe it's a bit later when the kids are finally in bed, and the first wave of silence settles over the house.

For me it was getting home from work, kicking my shoes off and immediately pouring a drink to help me relax. Then I would drink steadily as I stepped over the psychological threshold from work into evening, first prepping, then cooking and then eating dinner.

Whatever your version of The Witching Hour, this is when your brain expects alcohol, because this is when it's always been there. It's not just a craving; it's a deeply ingrained association. A well-worn mental path that has been reinforced over time.

But here's the important thing: it doesn't last all night. When I started changing my drinking behaviour, I realised that if I didn't drink by the time I had my dinner, then the chances are that I wouldn't then start. If I could ride out 6–8/8.30pm, then it could be a non-drinking evening. The urge would have somehow gone.

That realisation was a game-changer.

For most people, drinking is front-loaded into the early evening. And if you don't start, you're far less likely to crave it later on. If you can ride out those one or two hours. If you can push through without reaching for that first drink, then the urge will pass.

Instead of framing this as I have to go a whole day without drinking (which feels huge), reframe it as I only need to get through these next two hours.

Suddenly, the task at hand becomes much more focused.

Once you've identified your Witching Hour, you can use the wide range of little habit changes suggested in this chapter to begin to take back control – by switching up your routine, breaking old patterns and walking a different path through your evening.

KEY TAKE-AWAYS:

- Willpower fades – systems last. Relying on willpower alone is like running on a low battery; habit change needs structure, not strain.
- Don't fight a craving – reroute it. Replacing the old habit with a better response breaks the loop more effectively than resisting it.
- Small shifts beat big overhauls. Tiny, consistent changes bypass resistance and build momentum.
- Upgrade your self-care. New habits that nourish you will help fill the emotional and behavioural space alcohol used to occupy.
- Identity leads the way. Moving from 'I'm trying to cut back' to 'I'm someone who looks after myself' makes change stick.
- The Witching Hour is when drinking habits are strongest. Targeting this window can significantly disrupt ingrained patterns.

Food for thought: The Witching Hour challenge

Imagine you're climbing over a stile into a field of grass.

Healthy, green, knee-height grass fills the entire field. And there is one path from where you stand to the gate on the far side. A well-trodden, earth-brown channel, cut through the field, parting the grass on either side. The unquestionable route to follow. That path is the result of repeated use. It has been created by people walking down it. It only remains a path because it is used on a frequent basis. If all the local walkers woke up one morning and decided to walk a different way, they would start the creation of a different path, treading down the grass in a different direction which, over time, would become an established route through the field. And the original one? It would grow over. Eventually it would cease to be a path at all. Now apply that analogy to your evening routine. If you can walk a different path through your evening, from 6-8pm, you can form a new clear-cut alternative to what you've always done in the past.

Identify your Witching Hour
- What time of day is your strongest urge to drink?
- What usually triggers it? (Walking through the door? Cooking dinner? A feeling of stress?)
- How long does it last?

Map your current routine
- What do you usually do during this time?
- What drink do you normally reach for?
- What emotional state are you in before and after?

Create a disruption plan
- Change the setting: if you always drink in the kitchen, step outside, take a walk, or go to another room.
- Change the action: instead of reaching for a drink, what else could you put in your hand? A glass of

sparkling water? A cup of tea?
- Change the rhythm: if dinner prep triggers drinking, can you move dinner earlier, batch cook ahead of time, or change your evening flow?
- Insert a mood-boosting activity: try doing some exercise, take a hot bath, get absorbed in a book – anything that shifts your state without alcohol.

Make it a one-night experiment
- Tell yourself: 'I don't have to give up drinking forever. I just need to see what happens if I change things for one night.'
- Set yourself up for success by preparing alternatives ahead of time.
- Check in afterwards: did the urge pass? Did you feel better, worse, or just different?

Relevant podcast episodes:

Episode 10. Tools to Manage Habitual Evening Drinking
Episode 43. How Do I Cope with Setbacks?
Episode 50. Progress over Perfection – A New Approach to Dry January
Episode 54. Breaking the Alcohol Cycle – Habits vs Dependency
Episode 59. Practical Ways to Build Positive Habits
Episode 62. Our Alcohol Stories: Words that Can Change Your Life
Episode 68. 5-Minute Resets: Go-To Alternatives to Alcohol

CHAPTER 11

SACKING THE CEO

For years, decades even, alcohol has been sitting in the corner office, calling the shots on how you handle emotions. It's been the Chief Emotions Officer, making the big decisions in your life as to how to deal with stress, boredom, anxiety, sadness, even joy. Without realising it, you've let it run the show.

Hopefully you can now see that alcohol is a terrible CEO. It over-promises, under-delivers and operates purely on short-term gains. It convinces you it has everything under control while secretly running your emotional system into the ground. Instead of enabling you to learn to sit with discomfort, or understand what your emotions are actually trying to tell you, it just presses the mute button. Over and over again. And as an anaesthetic, it hasn't just been silencing pain. It's been dulling everything. It's like putting a dimmer switch on your entire emotional world. The highs aren't as high, the joys aren't as joyful, and the clarity you need to navigate life remains out of reach.

So, let's call this what it is: a redundancy notice: alcohol, you're fired.

But, if alcohol isn't the answer, what is?

YOU'RE HIRED!

Congratulations, you're taking over the role of CEO. And unlike alcohol, you're actually going to do the job properly. Yes, you're going to have to dig deep and do some work, because it's not a role you'll necessarily just slip into and conquer on day 1. But it's a job you'll excel at over time, as you build that life of 10/10s. Just remember your Wheel of Life and hold it as your vision – a clear and compelling image of a life you won't feel the urge to escape from. Here are some important principles to help you on your way:

1. Take ownership

It's easy to believe that our suffering is caused by external circumstances – the job, the relationship, the stress, the expectations. We think, if life were easier, I'd feel better. So we reach for alcohol to escape these pressures, convinced they're the problem. But taking ownership means recognising a deeper truth: it's not what happens to us that causes distress, but how we interpret and react to it.

- Stress at work doesn't force you to drink – the way you think about stress does.
- Loneliness doesn't make you pour a glass of wine – the way you process loneliness does.
- Frustration, boredom and sadness – they are not instructions to drink, but signals asking to be understood.

No one else is responsible for your emotional state. Not your boss. Not your partner. Not the traffic or the weather. And definitely not a bottle of wine. When you say:

- 'I am responsible for how I feel.'
- 'I can't control everything, but I can control how I respond.'
- 'If I don't like how I feel, I have the power to change it – not by avoiding it, but by understanding it.'

… You reclaim your agency. You stop feeling powerless and start living with intention. That's the difference between reacting and responding – between staying stuck and moving forward.

2. Stop with comparisons

We live in a world obsessed with what we're not. Social media, advertising and our culture of constantly having to 'keep up' convince us that our happiness is tied to how we measure up to others.

- I'm not as successful as them.
- I don't look like that.
- I should be further along.

Comparing ourselves to others is a happiness killer. It's the thief of joy.

What we could be celebrating about ourselves suddenly has the lustre removed when we spot someone else doing 'better'. It keeps us stuck in an endless loop of 'not enough'. The fresh perspective?

- There is no race.
- There is no finish line.
- You are exactly where you are meant to be.

Let go of judgement – of yourself, of others, of where you think you 'should' be by now. Because when you stop measuring your happiness against someone else's highlight reel, you free yourself to actually feel it.

3. Know your limits

This was a game-changer for me. Not because I suddenly had less to do, but because I stopped trying to control everything – including how I felt.

Like many high-functioners, I had internalised a lie: that happiness was something I had to earn through getting everything right. That if I looked a certain way, achieved enough and kept life 'together', then I'd finally feel good. And when I inevitably fell short of those impossible standards? I drank.

I drank to silence self-doubt. To smooth over the jagged edges of not-enoughness.

But happiness isn't found in perfection. It's found in presence – in being able to say this is hard and this is enough at the same time.

As Oliver Burkeman writes in *Meditations for Mortals*, peace doesn't come from finally getting everything under control – it comes from accepting that we never really will. His invitation is to stop striving for a life free of flaws or discomfort, and instead turn gently towards the chaos, the limits, the imperfections. To meet our limits with curiosity and compassion. Being human isn't a problem to solve – it's an experience to witness.

When I stopped thinking that I needed to 'fix' myself before I could feel good, something powerful shifted. I stopped chasing wholeness through performance. And I started finding it in the quiet relief of being instead of always *becoming*.

4. Embrace vulnerability as strength

We are often encouraged to keep it together. To soldier on. To bury our struggles under a smile. And then, when it all becomes too much, when the pressure builds, alcohol is there. A shortcut to relief. A way to exhale, without actually dealing with the weight we carry.

And yet real strength isn't putting on a brave face. Real strength is taking off the mask. Admitting when we're struggling. Being honest about how we feel and allowing ourselves to be fully seen.

Because happiness doesn't come from pretending life is perfect. It comes from embracing the truth – and knowing we are still enough.

5. Appreciate the now

Remember this one? We push happiness into the future, so that it's always one milestone away.

- I'll be happy when I lose 10lb.
- I'll be happy when I get the promotion.
- I'll be happy when I meet the right person.

As CEO, recognise that happiness is never 'there'. It's here. Not in some distant, perfected version of your life. But right now, in this moment, exactly as it is.

Incidentally, gratitude isn't just a cliché – it's a happiness amplifier. Because if you can't find joy in the small, imperfect, messy moments of today… you won't find it in some imagined future either.

6. Cultivate your inner mentor

We all have an inner voice – and for many of us, it's brutal.

- You're not good enough.
- You should be further along.
- You're failing.
- You're weak.

When that inner critic is in full flow, it's no wonder we reach for something to quiet the noise. But actually you don't need to silence that voice. You need to rewrite its script.

As CEO of your own life, you're allowed guidance – and there's no more powerful adviser than the one you consciously choose to cultivate: your inner mentor.

A voice that says:

- You're doing better than you think.

- You're allowed to be a work in progress.
- You're growing – even when it doesn't feel like it.

The way you speak to yourself shapes how you experience your life. So if happiness feels distant, maybe it's not your life that needs to change – but the voice narrating it.

WHEN THE NUMBING STOPS

What can you expect when you sack alcohol as CEO and take on the role yourself?

For so long, alcohol has been a buffer between you and your emotions. A filter that has softened the sharp edges of life. It hasn't just been something you drank. It has been something you used.

Many people assume that when they stop drinking, life just feels better. They picture themselves waking up refreshed, feeling lighter, more confident, more at peace. And while that's absolutely true in many ways, what they don't expect is this: it doesn't just feel better; it feels more.

When alcohol is no longer muting your emotions, everything gets louder. Stress isn't numbed. Anxiety isn't blurred at the edges. Self-doubt resurfaces, clearer than ever.

Can you remember times, maybe back when you were a child, when you were mucking around in a swimming pool, or the sea, and you tried to hold an inflatable ball under water? It took downward pressure, right? Quite a lot of it in fact. It was doable, but the ball squirmed as it tried to surface.

Then when you finally let go, and you let the ball take its natural trajectory, its flightpath could be both forceful and random. It shot up and went where it wanted to go.

Well that ball? That's the ball of emotions that you have used alcohol to suppress and 'hold under'. Perhaps for many, many years. And when you remove that downward pressure, you need to be prepared that those emotions will surface.

When people ask me what the best thing is about not drinking, I say feeling my emotions. And when they ask me what the most challenging thing is, I say feeling my emotions.

It is both glorious, and hard. That's why emotional growth is essential. Because removing alcohol is only the first step. Learning how to handle life without it? That's the real work.

This chapter is about learning to process life fully, instead of fast-forwarding through the hard parts.

WHY EMOTIONAL GROWTH IS HARD

Imagine your house has a leaky roof. Every time it rains, water drips through the ceiling, making a mess. Instead of fixing the roof, you just put out buckets to catch the water. It's a quick fix. It keeps the floors dry for now, but the leak never goes away. And over time, the damage gets worse. The walls start to dampen. They go mouldy. The floor timbers rot, and the very foundations weaken.

That's what drinking does. It catches the emotional

overflow of stress, anxiety, self-doubt and loneliness, without ever actually repairing the problem. It gives temporary relief, but the cracks are still there, growing beneath the surface.

When you stop drinking, it's like finally removing the buckets and looking up at the damage. It's uncomfortable, overwhelming, and tempting to just put the buckets back and pretend you never saw it.

Look at it this way, though: you were already working hard. You were already managing the leak, just in a way that kept you stuck. What if you put that same energy into building something better?

Now, you have a chance to fix the roof. To repair, rather than just react. And yes, it takes effort, but it also means you're building something solid. Something that will actually protect you, rather than something that will crumble and deteriorate over time.

What if, instead of just covering up discomfort, you actually built resilience? If, instead of avoiding pain because you felt it would break you, you found out you were stronger than you ever realised?

Emotions aren't problems to be fixed. They're experiences to be felt.

You don't need alcohol to get rid of uncomfortable feelings. You need the right tools to move through them, to process them, and to build the resilience that drinking never gave you.

YOUR EMOTIONAL TOOLBOX

When we've got an emotional problem, a difficult feeling, we don't tend to look for tools other than alcohol because, for so long, we haven't had to. It's everywhere, and so deeply embedded in our culture that we mistake it for a universal solution. Like an Inuk who believes the world is covered in snow, or a Saharan nomad who assumes the world is only sand, we grow up believing that alcohol is just what you do – to celebrate, to commiserate, to unwind, to belong. It becomes the default answer to every question, that Swiss Army Knife of emotional management.

But what if we've been looking at it all wrong? What if alcohol isn't the tool, it's just the most familiar one? And what if, just beyond the snow or the sand, there's an entire landscape of healthier, more effective tools waiting to be discovered?

Interestingly, many cultures around the world don't rely on alcohol as a primary coping mechanism. In Eastern traditions, where alcohol isn't embedded deeply in social rituals, people have developed alternative emotional management strategies. Ones that focus on inner balance, self-regulation and connection to something deeper.

For example, in Buddhist traditions, meditation and mindfulness have long been regarded as the best tools to manage suffering, a way of observing and accepting one's emotions rather than numbing them. In Japan, tea ceremonies serve as a practice of mindfulness and social connection, where presence and ritual replace the need for alcohol-fuelled bonding. In India, yoga and breathwork (pranayama) are ancient tools for managing emotions and stress.

These cultures show us something powerful. Alcohol is not a necessity for handling life. It's just one way that some societies have chosen to do it. And there are other, more effective, more fulfilling ways:

What alcohol provides	**What actually works better**
Relaxation after a stressful day	Breathwork and mindfulness
A confidence boost in social situations	Self-connection and reframing discomfort as excitement
A way to numb sadness, loneliness, or anxiety	Journalling, movement and self-inquiry
A reward after a tough day	Self-compassion and meaningful rituals

These alternative ways of managing emotions have been tested over centuries. They work. They don't just mask discomfort for a few hours. They transform your relationship with it. Let's be clear – I'm no Buddhist monk, and the closest I get to deep spiritual wisdom is watching Kung Fu Panda with a cup of tea. I don't wake up at dawn to meditate under a Bodhi tree, and my Downward Dog looks more like a collapsing deck chair. But here's the thing. I don't have to be a guru to borrow from these traditions. Over time, I've dialled into some of these tools – not in a perfectly enlightened way, but in a real-life, still-figuring-it-out kind of way. And what I've found is that they work. Not because they're mystical or exclusive, but because they give me something alcohol never did: a way to actually process emotions, instead of just drowning them in a glass of wine.

So I'm not here to play the role of a wise old sage (I can't actually sit cross-legged for more than five minutes without regretting many of my life choices), but what I can do is share what's actually helped me. Not theories, not abstract philosophies, but real, practical tools that I've tried, tested and – on most days – actually use.

These aren't about achieving some zen-like state of permanent bliss – I still lose my temper when Wi-Fi doesn't work. They're about giving yourself options. Because when you take alcohol off the table, you need something else in its place. Something that actually helps, rather than just numbs. And part of that 'something else' is understanding that it's not just about how you manage emotions *after* they hit. It's also about how you prevent emotional overload in the first place.

One thing I've come to realise, especially through my podcast conversation with Chloe Stephens, founder of A Flow Coach, is that many of us don't even realise how depleted we are from one day to the next. Chronic stress (and the negative thoughts it brings) doesn't always feel dramatic – it becomes our normal. Like a swan gliding smoothly while paddling frantically beneath the surface, we adjust to operating in overdrive without even noticing.

And when we finally do stop? We often mistake collapse – vegging out on the sofa, mindlessly scrolling, pouring a glass of wine – for recovery. But real recovery isn't about zoning out. It's about actively restoring the nervous system, quieting the mind, and giving ourselves permission to be still without guilt. Strategic recovery – simple acts like deep breathing, conscious pauses, and space from constant stimulation – isn't just self-care fluff. It's essential maintenance. Without it, we stay locked in a cycle of depletion, where alcohol feels like the only reliable off-switch.

We haven't just lost our ability to rest – we've forgotten that we even need to.

Here are the tools that I tap into to help me strengthen my emotional foundations before cracks appear *and* manage difficult feelings when they show up.

BREATHWORK: the fastest way to regulate emotions

Breathwork is one of the most effective ways to regulate emotions because it directly affects your nervous system.

When you drink to relax, you're relying on alcohol to artificially slow your heart rate and calm your mind. But your breath already has this power. It just needs to be activated.

The science behind breathwork
- Breathwork stimulates the vagus nerve, which shifts your body out of the fight-or-flight response and into a calm, relaxed state.
- Deep breathing lowers cortisol, the stress hormone, reducing anxiety in real time.
- Controlled breathing balances oxygen and carbon dioxide levels in the blood, preventing the light-headedness and tension often linked to stress and panic.
- Studies show that just two minutes of deep breathing can significantly lower your blood pressure and heart rate, mimicking the effects people seek from alcohol.

How to do it: a simple breathwork exercise
The box breathing technique:
- Inhale deeply through your nose for a count of 4.
- Hold your breath for a count of 4.
- Exhale slowly through your mouth for a count of 4.
- Hold again for a count of 4.
- Repeat for 2-3 minutes, or until you feel calmer.

Key takeaway
Breathwork is free (alcohol is not). It is instant (alcohol is

convenient, but not instant as such). And it is a scientifically backed tool for emotional regulation (alcohol, as we know, kick-starts an emotional rollercoaster). And unlike alcohol, it leaves you feeling better afterwards, not worse.

MINDFULNESS: The practice of noticing without reacting

Mindfulness is the antidote to autopilot drinking. When we drink to escape emotions, we're reacting rather than responding. We feel something uncomfortable, and we reach for a drink to suppress or distract ourselves from it. Mindfulness interrupts that cycle by helping us create space between what we feel and what we do next.

I'm not going to lie, I was a bit of a mindfulness sceptic, confusing it with full-on practices of meditation. And early attempts left me feeling pretty useless. I felt unable to switch my brain off even for a second or two, much less a few minutes. I'd start thinking about the online grocery, or what I was having for dinner – all thoughts tended to involve food – and I'd become incredibly frustrated and jack it in.

But the little mindfulness exercise suggested here requires nothing more than 'noticing', which even I could manage.

The science behind mindfulness

- Mindfulness activates the prefrontal cortex, the area of the brain responsible for self-awareness and impulse control. This helps you pause before reacting.
- Studies show that regular mindfulness practice reduces rumination, stress and anxiety, leading to a greater

sense of emotional stability.
- Practising mindfulness lowers activity in the amygdala, the brain's fear centre, reducing emotional reactivity.
- Research indicates that mindfulness increases dopamine and serotonin, the neurotransmitters associated with pleasure and well-being. This offers a natural alternative to the fleeting chemical rewards of alcohol.

How to do it: A simple mindfulness exercise
The 5-4-3-2-1 grounding technique:
   a) Name 5 things you can see around you.
   b) Identify 4 things you can touch.
   c) Notice 3 things you can hear.
   d) Acknowledge 2 things you can smell.
   e) Focus on 1 thing you can taste.

This simple exercise anchors you in the present moment, interrupting cravings and emotional overwhelm.

Key takeaway
Mindfulness doesn't remove discomfort; instead, it teaches you to sit with it, observe it, and ultimately realise that no emotion is permanent. And unlike alcohol, it leaves you feeling more in control, not less.

SELF-CONNECTION: Tuning into yourself, without distraction
Alcohol often serves as a buffer, not just between us and

discomfort, but between us and ourselves. When we drink, we override our internal signals, ignoring what we truly need in favour of a quick escape.

Self-connection is about reversing that pattern. It's about learning to check in with ourselves instead of checking out.

Many Eastern traditions prioritise self-connection through ritual, self-inquiry and intentional solitude. In Japan, for example, the concept of Ma ('the space between things') encourages moments of stillness to connect with inner wisdom. Similarly, Buddhist practices use silent reflection to deepen self-awareness.

By building self-connection, you learn to recognise your true emotional needs, not just react to cravings or urges.

The science behind self-connection
- Studies show that regular self-inquiry practices (journalling, reflection, quiet time) lower anxiety and increase resilience by allowing the brain to process emotions constructively.
- People who are more aware of what's going on inside their body – like their heartbeat, tension, or breathing – tend to feel more emotionally steady and are less likely to act on impulse.
- Neuroscientists have found that solitude and reflection activate the default mode network (DMN) – a part of the brain responsible for self-awareness and problem-solving.

How to do it: A simple self-connection exercise
The 3-question check-in:
   a) What am I feeling right now? (Emotionally and physically)
   b) What do I actually need? (Not as in what do I want, but what would truly serve me?)
   c) What small action can I take to meet that need?

This practice rebuilds the ability to listen to oneself. So instead of numbing discomfort with alcohol, we start responding to our real needs.

Key takeaway
Self-connection isn't about sitting alone with your thoughts. It's about actively tuning into yourself and becoming the kind of person who knows what they need and takes action to meet it.

JOURNALLING: Giving your emotions a voice instead of drowning them

Journalling has been one of the most powerful tools in my emotional toolkit – not because it magically fixes things, but because it gives me space to process, release and reflect. And it doesn't have to look like a leather-bound notebook and a perfect morning routine. For some people, journalling takes the form of voice notes, messy scribbles, or even blogging.

When I spoke to author Clare Pooley on the podcast, she described how writing her blog during her first alcohol-free year became a lifeline. She didn't know at the time it would become a brilliant book, *The Sober Diaries*. She was simply telling the truth as she lived it. Letting it out. Making sense of what she was going through, one post at a time.

Thinking of journalling as a private and solitary exercise can make it feel daunting, whereas Clare's story shows it can be dynamic, connecting and transformative. Whether you're sharing it publicly or keeping it just for you, the act of writing can be its own kind of clarity. A release valve. A witness. A way to stay connected to your 'why' when things feel foggy. When emotions stay locked in your head, they loop endlessly. Writing them down externalises them, which helps you gain clarity and relief.

The science behind journalling
- Emotional processing: studies show that expressive writing helps people make sense of their emotions, reducing stress and anxiety.
- Self-awareness: writing about experiences activates the prefrontal cortex, allowing for better decision-making instead of impulsive reactions.
- Mood regulation – journalling has been found to lower cortisol (the stress hormone), reducing the emotional weight of difficult experiences.

How to do it: A simple journalling exercise
The 'brain dump' method: there are scores of different ways to approach journalling, but this is great little starter.

a) Set a timer for 5 minutes.
b) Write whatever is in your head – without filtering, censoring, or overthinking. That bit is critical.
c) When the timer goes off, stop and re-read what you wrote.
d) Simply ask yourself: what is this telling me?

Key takeaway

Journalling isn't about writing well. It's about writing honestly. Getting emotions on to paper helps process them in a way that alcohol never could.

MOVEMENT: Releasing emotions instead of holding them in

Emotions aren't just thoughts, they live in the body. When you're stressed, you feel it in your tight shoulders. When you're anxious, your heart races. Movement releases these stuck emotions so they don't linger.

The science behind movement
- Physical release: exercise reduces cortisol and increases dopamine, making you feel calmer and more stable.
- Emotional processing: studies show that rhythmic movement (walking, dancing, yoga) activates the same brain regions as therapy, helping you work through emotions.
- Energy shift: moving your body shifts your nervous system out of fight-or-flight mode into a relaxed state.

How to do it: a simple movement exercise
The 'shake it off' method:
   a) Stand up and shake your arms, legs, shoulders for 30 seconds.
   b) Stretch or walk around for a few minutes.
   c) Notice if your mood or tension has shifted.

Key takeaway
Even very simple movement releases emotions. Just two minutes of moving your body can create a noticeable emotional shift.

SELF-INQUIRY: Understanding yourself instead of avoiding yourself

Alcohol often silences inner questions. When drinking, it's easy to avoid asking yourself: 'What do I really need? What am I feeling?' Self-inquiry reverses that pattern. It's the practice of getting curious about your emotions, behaviours and beliefs – without judgement.

The science behind self-inquiry
- Emotional awareness: research shows that reflecting on emotions reduces impulsivity and increases self-regulation.
- Cognitive reframing: self-inquiry helps shift limiting beliefs, creating new, healthier thought patterns.
- Mind-body connection: studies indicate that people who practise self-reflection experience lower stress and greater emotional stability.

How to do it: A simple self-inquiry exercise
The 'what's beneath this?' method:
   a) Identify a feeling (e.g. stress, frustration, loneliness).
   b) Ask yourself what's beneath this feeling? Keep asking until you uncover the root cause.
   c) Next ask what the feeling is trying to tell you? So, before rushing to fix it, pause here and consider what the emotion is asking you to acknowledge.
   d) Write down or say aloud the answer to the question 'What do I actually need?'

Key takeaway
Self-inquiry isn't about overthinking. It's about getting honest with yourself so you can meet your emotional needs in a healthier way.

SELF-COMPASSION: Changing the inner voice that fuels drinking

For many, alcohol is a way to quiet the inner critic. That voice that tells you you're not enough, that you've failed, that you need to escape. Without alcohol, that voice might feel louder at first. But the answer isn't drinking – it's changing the conversation in your head.

The science behind self-compassion
- Reduces self-criticism: research shows that self-compassion lowers negative self-talk and reduces shame – a major trigger for drinking.
- Increases resilience: studies indicate that people who

practise self-compassion recover faster from setbacks and are more likely to stick to positive habits.
- Regulates emotions: MRI scans show that self-compassion activates the same parts of the brain that create feelings of connection and safety.

How to do it: A simple self-compassion exercise
The 'talk to yourself like a friend' method:
a) Identify something you're beating yourself up about.
b) Imagine that a close friend was telling you they were struggling with the same thing.
c) What would you say to them? Now, say that to yourself.

Key takeaway
Self-compassion is not self-indulgence. The advice you give others is often so much more considered than the bullshit you fire at yourself. It's a way of treating yourself with the kindness you'd offer anyone else. And when you're kinder to yourself, you're far less likely to reach for alcohol to escape self-judgement.

MEANINGFUL RITUALS: Replacing alcohol with purposeful connection

Drinking is often ritualistic e.g. pouring a glass of wine at the end of a long day, clinking glasses in celebration, or holding a drink to feel part of a social occasion. But rituals don't need to involve alcohol to be powerful. Many cultures use rituals as a way to create connection, presence and emotional grounding. Rituals help mark transitions, provide comfort and make ordinary moments meaningful.

The science behind meaningful rituals
- Reduces stress: studies show that intentional rituals lower cortisol and increase feelings of stability and control.
- Creates social bonding: rituals provide a sense of community and belonging, reinforcing positive emotional connections.
- Increases mindfulness: engaging in slow, deliberate actions helps anchor the mind in the present moment, reducing anxious thoughts.

How to do it: Creating your own meaningful ritual
The 'mindful transition' method:
- a) Choose a specific moment you used to associate with alcohol (e.g. finishing work, a social gathering, winding down for the evening).
- b) Replace it with a ritual that engages your senses e.g. a beautifully brewed tea, lighting a candle, playing calming music, or even stepping outside for fresh air.
- c) Make it deliberate and enjoyable, just as you would savour a drink.

Key takeaway
Rituals provide emotional comfort and connection, without relying on alcohol. They remind us that meaning comes from the moment itself, not what's in our glass.

FINDING WHAT WORKS FOR YOU

What you use as a coping mechanism is deeply personal. As William Porter said when he came on the podcast: 'For me, particularly because of my time in the military, I exercise. Going for a run makes me feel better, more resilient. I like reading too. Losing myself in a book is almost like meditation. It gives my mind a break.'

And that's the point. Coping doesn't have to look like deep breathing on a mountaintop or hours of silent reflection (unless that's your thing, in which case go for it). It just has to be something that gives you a mental reset. Something that helps you shift gears after a stressful day, without relying on alcohol to do it for you.

For some, it's movement – running, yoga or dancing around the kitchen to an 80's playlist. For others, it's creativity – painting, knitting, journalling, playing an instrument. And sometimes, it's just simple pleasure – losing yourself in a book, watching a box set or calling a friend.

The key is this: find what works for you. Drinking has a way of shoving everything else aside, taking up time, headspace and energy. But when you step away from it, you get to reclaim that space. You get to rediscover the things that actually bring you joy, relief and a sense of balance.

A brilliant place to start is to therefore look back and ask yourself what you used to do? What brought you joy before drinking? In the opening chapter of this book, I mentioned that I loved art galleries. I also used to like long bike rides. Or cooking up a storm in the kitchen. All of these things are 'back on' once time has been reclaimed from drinking.

And the best part? Unlike alcohol, these things don't feel like coping mechanisms. They are just things I enjoy doing – that slipped by the wayside when I got side-tracked by alcohol. Things that nourish, instead of numb.

THIS WAS NEVER A 'HOW TO'. IT WAS A 'WHAT IF?'

This was never a 'how to' book. I didn't write it to tell you how to give up alcohol, or to insist that you must. Instead, it's been an invitation to step back, take an honest look, and ask yourself the only question that really matters: is my life as good as it could be?

Because what I've learned, and what I hope this chapter has shown you, is that emotional reliance on alcohol isn't just about drinking too much. It's about outsourcing your feelings, dampening your experience of life, and unknowingly handing over control to something that was never truly working for you.

But now you know different. You've seen what's possible when you reclaim your emotional world, and when you build a toolbox that actually helps you navigate life on your terms.

This being the case, the next question is not: 'Should I change?' but: 'Why wouldn't I?'

Because if there's ever been a better time to rethink your drinking, it's right now.

KEY TAKE-AWAYS

- Fire alcohol as your emotional CEO. It's been managing your feelings poorly for too long – numbing, distracting, but never resolving. It's time to reclaim the role.
- Awareness and ownership go hand in hand. Your emotions aren't dictated by external events – they're shaped by how you interpret and respond to them.
- Feeling more is part of healing. When you remove alcohol, emotions surface – but this is where true resilience is built.
- You need better tools, not more willpower. Breathwork, journalling, movement and self-connection offer real, lasting emotional relief.
- The goal isn't just drinking less – it's living more. This is about emotional autonomy, not abstinence. A full, vibrant life is the real reward.

Food for thought:

1. **What if feeling more (not less) was the key to everything you want?**
   How would your life change if you fully embraced your emotions instead of avoiding them?
2. **Have you been outsourcing your entire emotional well-being?**
   If alcohol isn't the answer, what tools and strategies could you use instead?
3. **What is your personal definition of emotional strength?**
   Does it involve hiding how you feel, or does it mean facing emotions head-on?

4. What small shifts could you make today to build a better emotional toolbox?

Whether it's movement, mindfulness, connection or creativity, think of one thing you could try.

5. Are you ready to take ownership of your emotions, once and for all?

If so, what's one immediate step you can take?

Relevant podcast episodes:

Episode 5. The Nation's Favourite Coping Mechanism – Explained

Episode 6. Taking Charge

Episode 20. Mindful Mastery: The Science & The Know-how

Episode 39: From Alcohol to Authenticity, with Clare Pooley

Episode 47. How Do I Deal With Really Low Moments?

Episode 49. Alcohol-free & Thriving: The Power of Positivity

Episode 53. Recapping on A Year of Tools

Episode 66. From Stress to Flow: Balance, Not Booze

Episode 67. Less Wine, More Oxygen: Breathwork for the Doubtful Drinker

Episode 68. 5-Minute Resets: Go-to Alternatives to Alcohol

CHAPTER 12

WHAT ARE YOU THIRSTY FOR?

Something is happening.

For the first time in history, the old, unquestioned narratives about alcohol are starting to crack. The tide is turning. The love affair is losing its sparkle. And people everywhere are beginning to wonder: Do I really need this? Is alcohol giving me what I think it is?

Maybe you've felt it too. That quiet awareness creeping in. The sense that the grip alcohol has had (on your life, your social circles, maybe even your identity) just isn't as tight as it once was.

If so, you are not alone. In fact, you are right on time.

Because this isn't just a personal shift. It's a cultural one.

THE BLINKERS ARE COMING OFF

For decades, our 'love affair' with alcohol, the one that Professor David Nutt and I spoke about, has been blind. Blind because we were so in love we never questioned it. Blind because we overlooked its flaws, its deceptions, its harms. Blind because it was woven into the fabric of our lives so tightly that the idea of not drinking felt almost… unthinkable.

To refuse alcohol was to make a statement, one that risked being met with scepticism, discomfort or outright ridicule. If you weren't drinking, people assumed there was a reason. And by 'reason', they meant a 'problem'.

But something's changing.

People are waking up to the fact that alcohol has never been just a social lubricant, a stress reliever, or a harmless indulgence. It's a drug. And it's been marketed to us as something far safer, far more glamorous and far more essential than it actually is.

And now?

More and more people are stepping back and seeing alcohol for what it really is. What's more, they're making a conscious decision to drink less or not at all. Simply because they want to.

The proof is everywhere. You just need to look around to see the evidence of this evolution:

- **The rise of sober-curious movements.** From Sober October to Dry January and beyond, choosing to drink less is no longer just for people with 'a problem'. It's a mainstream conversation.
- **Celebrities and influencers are normalising alcohol-free lifestyles.** Far from being a shameful secret, not drinking is becoming aspirational.
- **Mental health awareness is at an all-time high.** The spotlight has been well and truly shone on mental

health in the last four to five years, illuminating the negative impact of alcohol. More people are realising that alcohol isn't just numbing the bad feelings, it's actually creating them.
- **The explosion of alcohol-free alternatives.** Go into any supermarket, and you'll see it: entire shelves dedicated to alcohol-free wines, beers and spirits. Even the biggest alcohol brands are hedging their bets. They know the tide is turning.

All of this is creating a new landscape. One where drinking is no longer the default, where alcohol is just an ingredient and where questioning whether you want it in your drink marks you out as being aware, not weird.

This matters, because the more we normalise questioning alcohol, the more space we create for others to do the same – without stigma, without judgement, and without fear.

And that's why your own Big Drink Rethink isn't just about you. It's about being part of something bigger.

Because real change always starts with the individual. And when enough of us start asking different questions, the world around us has no choice but to evolve.

What this means for you

So, here you are.

You've seen the shift happening. You've questioned the old stories about alcohol. Maybe, for the first time, you've started to wonder: what if I don't need this? What if life could be better without it?

This is your moment.

And that's the most important thing. It's yours.

No one is telling you what to do. No one is making you choose. The only person who gets to decide what role alcohol plays in your life is *you*. And that's the most liberating part.

Let's step away from labels, rules and expectations for a second.

Forget the 'shoulds'. Forget what anyone else thinks.

Instead, ask yourself:

- Is alcohol truly adding to my life?
- If I stopped drinking, what might I gain?
- If I could have all the confidence, connection and relaxation that alcohol promises – without the downside – would I take it?

These aren't trick questions. They are an invitation. A chance to get curious, not about alcohol itself, but about you.

The chances are you didn't pick up this book because you necessarily wanted to quit drinking. You picked it up because something inside you was looking for something, a change of perspective. More clarity. More presence. More truth. More *freedom*.

Maybe alcohol has been standing in the way of that. Maybe it hasn't. Only you know the answer.

But here's what I do know.

For years, I reached for alcohol thinking it would give me something – be it relief, connection, confidence, escape. But it never really gave me those things. Not in a lasting way. I was left chasing the same feeling again and again.

When I finally stopped drinking, I realised I hadn't been craving alcohol. I'd been craving something deeper.

- I wanted to feel comfortable in my own skin, without needing a drink in my hand.
- I wanted to build real confidence, without relying on artifice.
- I wanted to experience life fully, without blurring the edges.

And once I saw that, the question wasn't: 'Should I stop drinking?'

It was: 'Why wouldn't I?'

A NEW KIND OF CHOICE

For so long, drinking has felt like the default. Something we do without thinking, simply because everyone else does it too.

But the most powerful thing you can do, to be self-determining in your life, is to not follow the default, but choose for yourself.

What if, instead of asking, can I live without alcohol?, you asked:

- Who do I want to be?
- What kind of life do I actually want?
- Does alcohol help me get there – or hold me back?

At this point, there's nothing left to tell you. No instructions, no rules, no 'right' way forward. Just a simple truth: you have a choice.

Not the kind of choice that feels like an ultimatum. Not the kind that comes with pressure, sacrifice or struggle.

This is a different kind of choice – the kind that opens doors instead of closing them.

You've already mapped out what a 10/10 life could look like – the life designed by you, not one you simply slip into out of habit.

So, what if, just for a moment, you allowed yourself to wonder? What if you gave yourself the space to see what's possible?

WHAT ARE YOU THIRSTY FOR?

What if you allowed yourself the chance to experience life with full clarity, presence and power?

What if you stopped thinking of alcohol as something to give up. And started seeing what you might gain? Because the truth is you were never really thirsty for alcohol. You were thirsty for something deeper.

And now?

Now, you get to go and find it.

Because this was never really about drinking.

This was always about you.

ACKNOWLEDGEMENTS

This book was not written alone.

To the team at New River: thank you for believing in this idea, and in me. Rebecca – your early championing of this message gave it wings. Aurea – your editorial clarity, patience and gentle craftsmanship have made this book infinitely stronger. Ella & Katherine – if this book is in the hands of readers, it's because your marketing skills have made it travel far further than I ever could. Thank you.

To Phoebe and Claire at Winter Audio – the powerful sister-act who help me bring The Big Drink Rethink podcast to life: thank you for helping me give voice to the ideas and the stories that gave this book its heartbeat. And of course to every guest, who has shared their insight, experience and expertise on the podcast – your honesty, courage and generosity have helped reframe the conversation around alcohol, and I'm endlessly grateful. Long may it continue!

To Hannah Wilson, whose illustrations pepper these pages: thank you for capturing the complex with charm and simplicity.

To my friend (and often my coach) Lorna Wilson: for

calling me out, calling me forward, and daring me to 'play big'.

To my dear friend Gemma Atkinson-Brown: thank you for being my cheerleader-in-chief and my sounding board – from the birth of the podcast to the writing of these pages, you've believed in The Big Drink Rethink.

To my family, of course: thank you for giving me the time, space and encouragement to explore what matters most. Kieran – thank you for your steadiness and patience. Freya & Molly – thank you for the best reminder of what it means to live creatively and curiously.

And finally, to you, the reader: this book is for all of you asking the bigger questions. May it help you listen closely and uncover not just what you want less of… but what you are truly thirsty for.

NOTES

NOTES

NOTES

NOTES

NOTES

NOTES

NOTES

NOTES

NOTES

NOTES

ABOUT THE AUTHOR

Anna Donaghey is an alcohol mindset coach, speaker and host of The Big Drink Rethink, a podcast aimed at encouraging people to talk openly and honestly about alcohol which has had high profile guests. With a career spanning 25 years as a strategist in the advertising industry, she combines her own lived experience of alcohol addiction with great insight into what makes us tick and what influences us to behave the way we do. This is her first book. She lives with her family near Bristol.

Connect with Anna:
You can email Anna: **anna@thebigdrinkrethink.com**
Visit her website to explore how you can work with Anna to rethink your drinking: **thebigdrinkrethink.com**
Subscribe to **The Big Drink Rethink** podcast on any platform where you listen to shows.
Follow Anna on Instagram at **instagram.com/bigdrinkrethink**
And on Facebook at **facebook.com/thebigdrinkrethink**